# D▲Da PRESENTISM

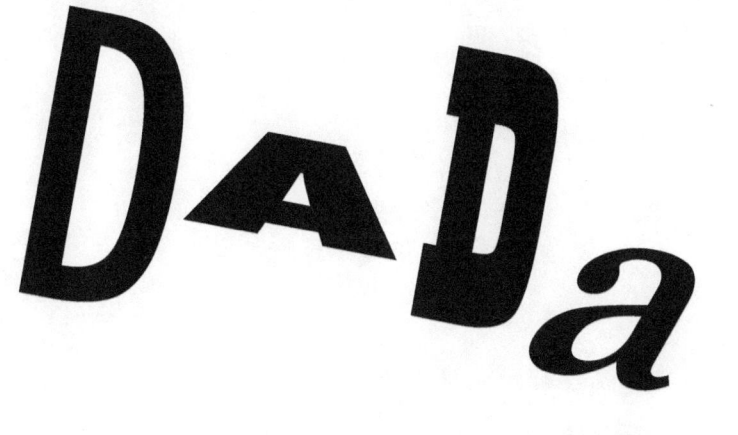

# PrEsEnTiSm

## AN ESSAY ON ART & HISTORY

MARIA STAVRINAKI

TRANSLATED BY
Daniela Ginsburg

Stanford University Press
STANFORD, CALIFORNIA

The French manuscript has been translated thanks to the support of the Gerda Henkel Stiftung.

Printed in the United States of America on acid-free, archival-quality paper

Library of Congress Cataloging-in-Publication Data

Stavrinaki, Maria, author.
Dada presentism : an essay on art and history / Maria Stavrinaki ; [translated by] Daniela Ginsburg.
    pages cm
Translated from the French.
Includes bibliographical references and index.
ISBN 978-0-8047-9424-4 (cloth : alk. paper)—
ISBN 978-0-8047-9812-9 (pbk. : alk. paper)—
ISBN 978-0-8047-9815-0 (electronic)
1. Dadaism—Germany—Berlin. 2. Arts, Modern—20th century. 3. Arts and history. I. Title.
NX550.B4S73 2016
709.04'062—dc23
    2015028116

Designed by Bruce Lundquist

Typeset at Stanford University Press in 11/15 Adobe Garamond

For Alexis

# CONTENTS

## ACKNOWLEDGMENTS

This English translation of my French manuscript was made possible by the Gerda Henkel Stiftung; I would like to thank everyone who has supported the project.

This book owes a great deal to my discussions with Éric Michaud, and I would like to extend special thanks to Lisa Florman.

# DaDa PResEnTiSm

## ORLANDO

> For some seconds the light went on becoming brighter and brighter, and
> she saw everything more and more clearly and the clock ticked louder and
> louder until there was a terrific explosion right in her ear. Orlando leapt as
> if she had been violently struck on the head. Ten times she was struck. In
> fact it was ten o'clock in the morning. It was the eleventh of October. It was
> 1928. It was the present moment.
>
> —**Virginia Woolf**, *Orlando* (1928), **p. 224**

**ON THIS OCTOBER MORNING IN 1928**, after having crossed centuries
and continents, Orlando finds herself abruptly thrown into the present.
The 36-year-old woman that Virginia Woolf depicts, who first appears as
a young man in the Elizabethan era, sword playing in his ancestral home,
is now disconcerted by the displays in a London department store. The
agglomeration of goods in space is an exact expression of her experience
of time, for it is as though the moments she has lived, scattered across
centuries, are condensed into the hollow of the present. Each one of
Orlando's reincarnations throughout the ages reveals a new aesthetic to
her, an aesthetic not limited to art or the ordinary objects of everyday life
but one that touches on her perception and experience of the world. Just

as Oscar Wilde said about the fog that the Impressionists "introduced"[1] through their paintings of London, Orlando observes that at the beginning of the nineteenth century, the English climate has become significantly more humid, causing forms and colors to lose much of the solidity and clarity that had characterized them in the previous century. But in none of her projections into history's successive presents has the present imposed itself as violently as it does at that moment, like an explosion threatening at every instant to tear apart her being. The precision of her perception becomes more and more unbearable.

The involuntary and vexed empathy that Orlando feels toward the world she is discovering results from the fact that this latest present is also that of her author. The fact that the past presents have succeeded one another attenuates their unsettling uniqueness, but the time opened by Woolf's writing gapes wide, and its vast possibilities only sharpen the uniqueness of the current present: "Every time the gulf of time gaped . . . some unknown danger might come with it."[2] Furthermore, the current present, with its syncopated cadence and the shattering of perception that this entails—"What was seen begun . . . was never seen ended"[3]— seems more than ever before to favor the shattering of the self. Bringing the sequence of Orlando's past selves to an end, the present no longer guarantees the identity of the name Orlando, and it unbinds all the selves that this name has contained over the course of time.

It is only at dusk on that day of October 11, 1928, that Orlando finds peace. When the light of the setting sun begins to blur forms, colors, and sounds, she is once again able to find the indistinctness of time that has composed her life until that point; her memories and dreams, which seem to her also to be the raw material of art, chase away the brutality of the present. "It was the present moment," writes Woolf, recalling the beginning of that day; "what more terrifying revelation can there be than that it is the present moment? That we survive the shock at all is only possible because the past shelters us on one side, the future on another."[4]

# POSTHISTORY AND PREHISTORY

## Voluntary Contraction in the Present:
## Decision and Heroism

It was that same crepuscular protection provided by the past and future together that Dada refused when it in turn found itself projected into its own present, in the midst of the Great War. Richard Huelsenbeck, in importing the word *Dada* from Zurich to Berlin, contributed in many different ways to creating a constellation of artists grouped around that name. In his April 1918 Dadaist manifesto, he wrote:

> Art in its execution and direction is dependent on the time in which it lives, and artists are creatures of their epoch. The highest art will be that which in its conscious content presents the thousandfold problems of the day, the art which has been visibly shattered by the explosions of the last week, which is forever trying to collect its limbs after yesterday's crash. The best and most extraordinary artists will be those who every hour snatch the tatters of their bodies out of the frenzied cataract of life, who, with bleeding hands and hearts, hold fast to the intelligence of their time.[1]

For Huelsenbeck, holding fast to one's own time took a certain physical, intellectual, and moral courage and was even proof of heroism— albeit a heroism diametrically opposed to the kind that for the past four years had been required on the battlefield in the name of the eternity of nations. Against this mythical eternity, which produced nothing but the catastrophe of history—war—Dadaist heroism threw itself into the present, which, exactly because it was uncertain, seemed to be the only type of time favorable to the exercise of freedom. Only the present could allow another history to surge up, a history emancipated from servile obedience to the past and the chaste utopia of the future.

It was not the sentiment of transition in the strict sense of the word that characterized Dada's conception of its historical belonging—not, at least, in the sense of a bridge connecting the past to the future. Instead, the zone these artists inhabited was cut off and suspended; it was a narrow plank, hazardous terrain. In 1916, when the name *Dada* was first pronounced at the Cabaret Voltaire in Zurich, giving nominal unity to the multiform, if not disparate, activities that took place within its walls (poetry recitals, musical performances, songs, dances, performance art *avant la lettre*, and plastic productions of all kinds), these artists were aware that their "space of experience" and "horizon of expectation" had been seriously jarred. These two metahistorical categories were developed by the historian Reinhart Koselleck during the 1970s, and they account for an underlying process inherent in the modern conception of history: the acceleration of time that resulted from the human belief in the feasibility and perfectibility of history, beginning with the French Revolution, and systematically led to the shrinking of experience, which was replaced by an enlarged horizon of expectation. Encouraged by the philosophy of history and rationalist theories of progress, this projection in advance of the future implied that the present was inadequate to any experience transmitted by the past and was perhaps even incapable of generating its own experiences: "This accelerated time, i.e., our history, abbreviated the space of experiences, robbed them of their constancy, and continually brought into play new, unknown factors, so that even the actuality or complexity of these unknown quantities could not be ascertained."[2]

In a now famous essay from 1933, "Experience and Poverty," Walter Benjamin observed that World War I was a crucial cause of the present's elusiveness. The experience of the front, where technology had finally replaced humans on the field of battle, devalued all previously acquired experience—leaving recognizable only the clouds in the sky, as Benjamin put it—and in turn became incommunicable.[3] Many artists sought to repress this muteness and sublimate it in inaugural language; in a move typical of the apocalyptic dialectical conversion of catastrophe into benediction, they dreamt of erecting modern cathedrals on the fields of ruins. For these artists—for example, the Expressionists and Futurists—the pulverized past made it all the more easy to construct a hypertrophied future.[4] Their reaction fit perfectly within the temporal dynamic described by Koselleck.

But there were also artists for whom the view from the field of ruins revealed a blocked horizon. Such were the Dadaists. For Huelsenbeck—who was not only an actor in the Dada movement but also its urgent and assiduous historiographer—it was already clear in 1920 that Dada had developed in an age that presented intellectuals with "a large and difficult task," in that it was "harder than in quiet times to balance out the measure of personality and establish the orbit from which one [could] grow up as a self-possessed presence."[5] Of predecessors and tradition, nothing remained; these could neither accelerate nor hinder the course of things.[6] As for the future, various activists thought that they could remedy the collapse of the notion of *historia magistra vitae* (history as life's teacher) with the belief that history was on their side. But for Huelsenbeck, if history had a lesson to teach, it was that of its contingence or, worse, its impassive identity.[7] For those intellectuals and artists who found comfort neither in the past nor in the future, the only remaining choice was to gain a foothold in the present, which was by definition fleeting and more threatening than ever.

At bottom, all modernity was a challenge to the present; the fact that it was haunted by nostalgia for the past and an obsession with the future was in fact resounding proof of this challenge. Modernity was marked by moments of crisis, moments such as the years surrounding the Great War, which contracted into a single present, usually involuntarily, as for Orlando, and sometimes deliberately, as for Dada. François Hartog, in his study of the presentism of modernity, pursued Koselleck's hypotheses and found that, in the contemporary temporal configuration,

> the distance between the space of experience and the horizon of expectation has been stretched to its limit, to its breaking point, with the result that the production of historical time seems to be suspended. Perhaps this is what generates today's sense of a permanent, elusive, and almost immobile present, which nevertheless attempts to create its own historical time.[8]

Contemporary presentism's quest to produce its own historical time is haunted by commemoration of the past, which is more ghostly than ever. This mournful, obsessive fear of the past is one of the major differences between today's presentism and Dadaist presentism, which was highly festive in nature. Although the present, which rules absolutely, as Hartog writes, is obsessed with the duty to remember and a respect for heritage, Dadaist presentism revolted against any commemorative appropriation of a flawlessly coherent history. The two presentisms—the Dadaists' and ours—correspond to two completely different "regimes of historicity."[9] The present defended by Dada—by its Berlin contingent at least—was a truly revolutionary time, a "time filled by the presence of the now [*Jetztzeit*]," to use Walter Benjamin's expression; it was "a present which is not a transition, but in which time stands still and has come to a stop."[10] This present methodically deconstructed the historical, economic, and political method of capitalization instituted by German historicism; it did this through a series of precise formal mechanisms and an astonishing philosophical and political argument. As for our own dilated present, it is the expression of an age in which capitalism is hegemonic and revolution as a collective form for the suspension of time seems to belong to the annals of history.

As Huelsenbeck wrote:

> No one knows if he will be hit by the wave created by the raging storm at the other end of the world. The nerve-wracking uncertainty is the grisliest tool of the time, a truly demonic device of the machine age. Death approaches and none can look it in the eye; courage in the old sense is in decline; but here and there heroism is blazing and cries its old song of

defiance with which humanity has again and again wrested the justifica-
tion of its being.[11]

This book is dedicated to the Dadaists' heroic presentism in the face of a
simultaneous world that spared none and a history whose infernal repeti-
tion took away human freedom. To the Dadaists, heroic appropriation
of the present bore the ontological weight of a *decision*—the only intel-
lectually and ethically worthy one. But precisely because their presentism
involved a decision, it also promised an alternative, perhaps more cred-
ible, conception of the future.

Broadly, the Dadaists' decision to seize the present came out of their
rejection of both the historical past and a meliorist future whose exact
symmetry was confirmed in the parallel ways they instrumentalized the
present.[12] "The Dada person recognizes no past which might tie him
down," Raoul Hausmann wrote. "He is held up by the living present, by
his existence."[13] The Dadaists inherited their vitalist independence with
respect to the historical past from the Expressionists. All the pictorial
avant-gardes of the prewar era shared the view of history as a "burden,"
which Hayden White identified more generally in early twentieth-
century literature.[14] This history, seen either as a mechanical accumulation of events succeeding one another in time or as a reservoir of fixed
forms fashioned by the past and then erected into models, was violently
rejected by artists in the name of their *antimimetic* stance toward life.
Kurt Pinthus, man of letters and the author of an illuminating text on
Expressionist temporalities, wrote in 1919 that the past "lies behind us
untransformable, already."[15] And what this historicism was to the past,
meliorism was to the future: the two presupposed the same reproductive
and cumulative understanding of time. The past was the temporal aspect
of a passive reality—an ontological, artistic, social, and political reality—
that those enraged idealists, the Expressionists, wanted to combat so as to
shape it according to the requirements of their spirit.

The heroic overtones of Expressionist idealism aside, the Dadaists did
not disagree with the Expressionists' rejection of a fossilized past. What
distinguished the two movements was the way they correlated present

and future. Whereas the Dadaists wanted to achieve self-possession in the here and now, even in the face of adversity, Expressionist artists were "enem[ies] of the present," as Siegfried Kracauer put it in 1918.[16] To an Expressionist like Pinthus, the present, the quintessence of alienated time (which the Impressionists were mad enough to have elevated into the sole subject of their art), was "a furtively receding nothing."[17] "Only the future is entirely our work," he concluded, as though the only work the Expressionists were sure of having was the work they had not yet accomplished.[18] This projection into an indefinite future was the modern, optimistic, and historically confident version of the famous Pascalian dictum, "We never live, but hope to live."[19]

When it came to highlighting the historical legitimacy of their art and thereby the objectivity of their methods, Expressionist artists thus emphasized the fertility of their age, which they depicted as pregnant with the future. Expressionism had an intermediary temporal status that was explicitly expressed in its forms. As Jean-Claude Lebensztejn explained, the action of colors in Expressionist works was often dissociated from that of lines, and composition straddled abstraction and imitation. But it was above all the principle of dissonance or contrast that manifested Expressionism's intermediary system, a system whose entire meaning was based on an apocalyptic temporality. If the unusual and thereby shocking relationships between colors and forms did harm to the spectator's perception, it was so that it might later do good to his or her soul.

This belief in salvation through destruction translated, of course, into the spatial construction of the paintings, which, through the centrifugal tension that often organized them, signified the immanent destruction of inert matter through the creative force of subjectivity.[20] "Today," announced Franz Marc in 1912, "art is moving in a direction toward which our fathers would never even have dreamed. One stands before the new works as in a dream and hears the horsemen of the Apocalypse in the air. An artistic tension is felt all over Europe."[21] Wassily Kandinsky observed that in the two years separating the first and second editions of the *Blaue Reiter Almanach* (1912–1914), historical time noticeably contracted: "In the course of these two years we have come closer to the future."[22] This acceleration, which fits the mold of apocalyptic awaiting, whether properly religious or secularized,[23] can be seen in many of Marc's and Kandinsky's works; the taut convexity of their compositions suggests imminent explosion, like an egg on the verge of hatching life (Figure 1). Kandinsky formulated this thesis in *The Spiritual in Art* without the slightest ambiguity: "Art [that] has no power for the future, which is only a child of the age and cannot become a mother of the future, is a barren art."[24]

Whereas Expressionism's vocation was to give birth to the future, Dadaist practices were defined as children of the present. As we will see, the Dada artists had a different view of genealogy and a different idea of the relationship between forebears and posterity, progenitors and descendants, artists and works. As the architect and adroit observer Ludwig Hilberseimer wrote, they believed that "the true work of art will always be born only from the chaos of time."[25] Within this chaos, the end of time existed side by side with new possibilities, but these were possibilities *that began in the now*, from a new time. The role of the artist was to forge practices that would reveal the profound ambiguity of the present. This is why such contradictory tactics as eclecticism and primitivism, parody and utopia, were all used in Dadaism as equally appropriate responses. For these artists the future was not to come; it had already arrived.

## The Dadaist Present:
## A Mix of Historicism and Primitivism

It is not insignificant that Dada was invented in a cabaret, where the most historically and formally heterogeneous modes of expression could exist side by side. This did not escape the linguist Roman Jakobson, who in 1921 wrote a brief, but incisive text on Dada.

> During the last decade, no one has brought to the artistic market so much varied junk of all times and places as the very people who reject the past. It should be understood that the Dadaists are also eclectics,

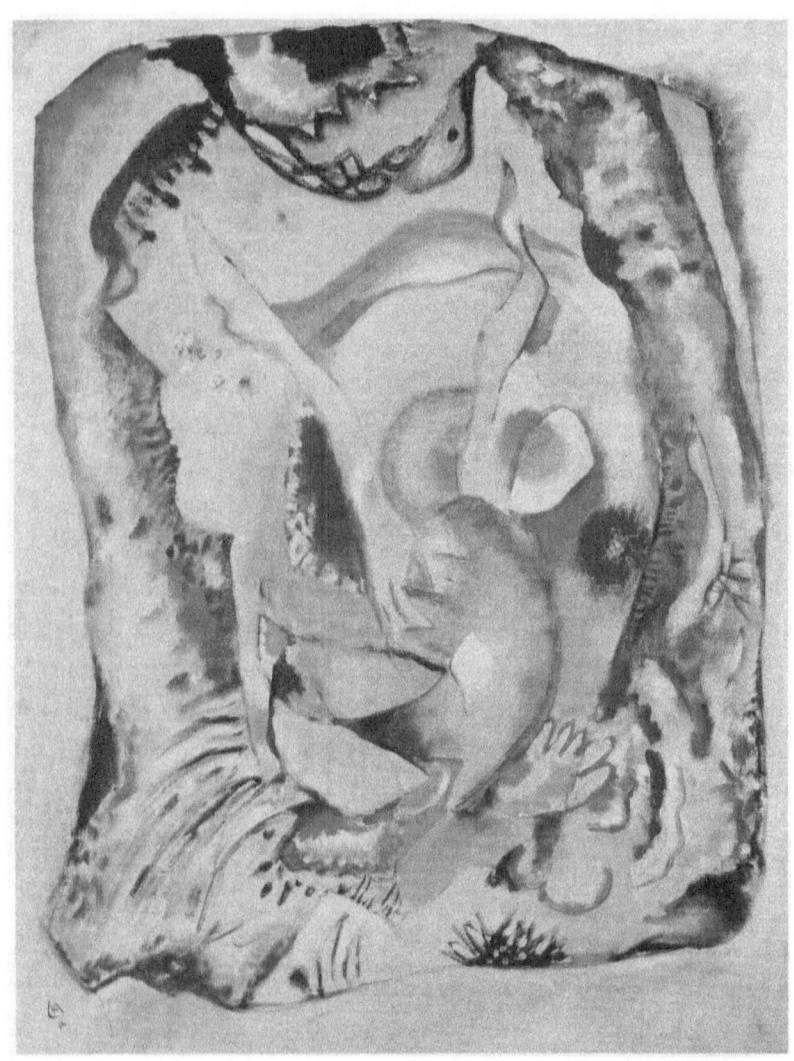

**FIGURE 1.** W. Kandinsky, *Tableau sur fond clair* (*Auf hellen Grund*), 1916, oil on canvas, 100 × 78 cm; MNAM, Donation Nina Kandinsky, Paris. Source: Catalog Wassily Kandinsky, MNAM, 1916.

though theirs is not the museum-bound eclecticism of respectful venera-
tion, but a motley café *chantant* program (not by chance Dada was born
in a cabaret in Zurich).[26]

Indeed, Huelsenbeck described the Cabaret Voltaire as "a catch-all for
the most diverse directions in art, which at that time seemed to us to
constitute 'Dada.' None of us suspected what Dada might really become,
for none of us understood enough about the times."[27] Hugo Ball, describing an evening at the Voltaire, wrote in his journal that "all the styles
of the last twenty years came together yesterday."[28] This eclectic logic,
which, in the absence of any notion of what a "proper" work might be,
turned to the works of others, was pursued in Berlin. In one of the many
roles they played between 1918 and 1920, John Heartfield and George
Grosz presented themselves as decorators who could create costumes and
décors in any style, in the fashion of any ism.[29]

In short, the Dadaists openly gave themselves over to an activity
that the nineteenth century had pursued with a blind frenzy. One of the
Dadaist responses to the failure of *historia magistra vitae* was to parody
that century's drive to devour history. Huelsenbeck, citing a few lines of
*Beyond Good and Evil* in the *Dada Almanac*, confirmed the Dadaist debt
to Friedrich Nietzsche's critique of historicism.

> Time and again a new piece of antiquity and foreign country is tried
> on, put on, taken off, packed away and above all *studied*:—we are the
> first studied period *in puncto* "costumes," by which I mean moralities,
> articles of faith, tastes for art and religion, prepared as no period before
> us for the carnival of great style, for spiritual carnival laughter and high
> spirits, for transcendental heights of the highest nonsense and Aristo-
> phanean mockery of the world. Perhaps we will discover right here the
> realm of our *invention*, that realm where even we can still be original,
> perhaps as parodists of world history and buffoons of God—perhaps,
> even if nothing else of today has a future, our *laughter* still has a future![30]

And indeed, laughter did have a future: Dada paradoxically drew a good
deal of its avant-garde originality from its satirical imitation of history.

In its desire to take on what the nineteenth century had endeavored to repress, Dadaist heroism moved into a space where the comic, fully assumed, turned tragic. As Huelsenbeck explained, "[We live in] times that, in their contrariness and in their obstinacy, have become almost a heroic gesture."[31]

It is also true that Dadaist heroism expressed itself *at the same time* in a fierce primitivism.[32] But it is important to emphasize that this primitivism was above all a presentism impatient to be lived rather than the regressive pursuit of an Edenic, purified future. As such, Dadaist primitivism was generally expressed through two different strategies: on the one hand, a strategy of abstraction (pictorial abstraction for someone like Hans Arp; poetic abstraction in the work of someone like Hugo Ball), which sought to grasp the immediate elementariness of life;[33] and on the other hand, a strategy of deliberate, and clearly more historicized, empathy with the manifestations of an adverse present, especially among the Dadaists of Berlin, Cologne, and Paris. Like Wilhelm Worringer, the Dadaists attributed a prophylactic function to abstract primitivism. But during this period, in which the Greek ideal was replaced by alternative models from other cultures with their own techniques of mediation (whether real or imagined), empathy was diverted from its naïve context in Worringer's theory and took on a properly apotropaic aim.[34]

For Hugo Ball, what was most incredible "in the midst of enormous unnaturalness" was "the direct and the primitive."[35] In his journal he reported Arp's irritation with the Expressionist ideology visible in Franz Marc's paintings. Arp contrasted Marc's "painted versions of the Creation and the Apocalypse" with the "plane geometry" of his own compositions.[36] This plane geometry, like its opposite, the random order of his torn-paper works, spatially expressed the present—not the concrete present of history but the eternal and impassive present of nature (Figure 2).[37] It was this *equality of time* that was to replace Marc's animal primitivism and sacrificial apocalypse (Figure 3). Years later, Hans Arp explained that the abstract forms he and Sophie Täuber created during their Dada years "were supposed to be freed of passions, torments, and

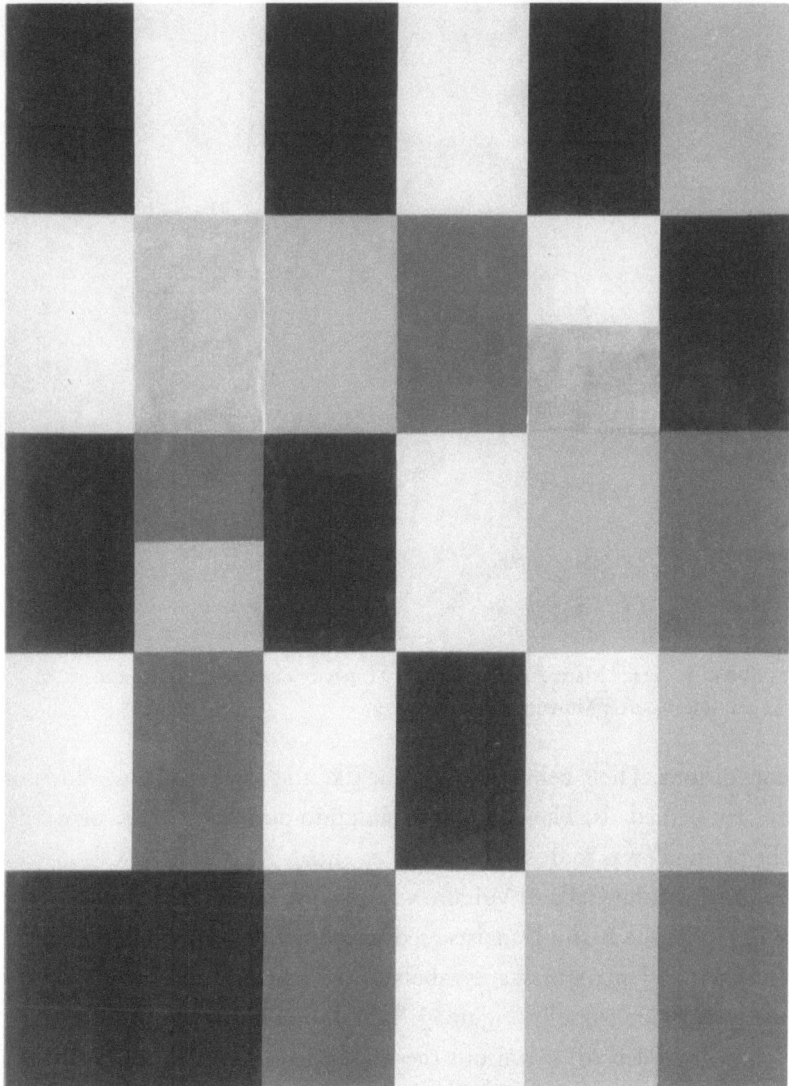

**FIGURE 2.** Hans Arp and Sophie Täuber, *Untitled* (*Duo-Collage*), 1918, paper, board, and silver leaf on board, 82 × 62 cm (32 ¹⁄₁₆ × 24 ⁷⁄₁₈ inches); Staatliche Museen zu Berlin, Nationalgalerie. Source: Catalog Dada, National Gallery of Art, Washington, 2006. © ADAGP, Paris 2015.

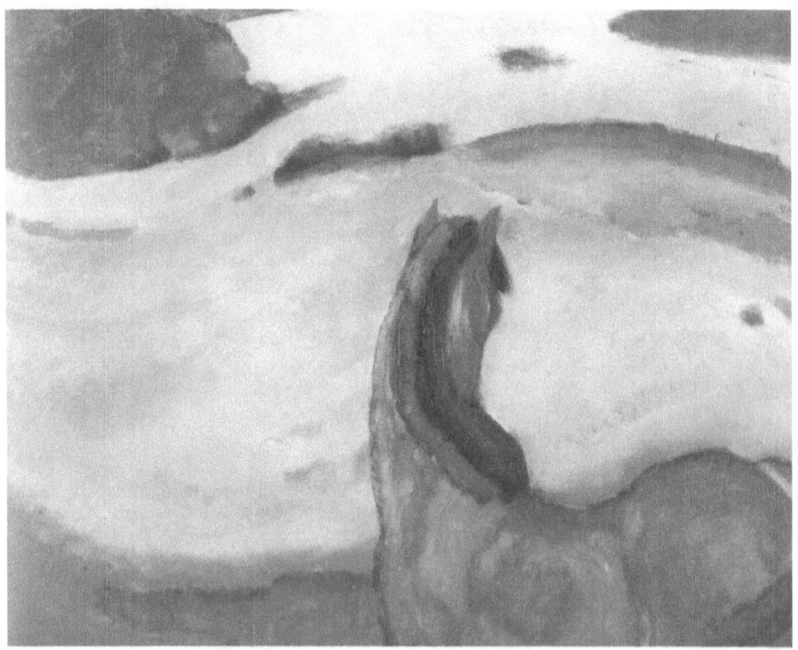

**FIGURE 3.** Franz Marc, *Horse in Landscape* (*Pferd in Landschaft*), oil on canvas, 80 × 112 cm, 1910. Source: Museum Folkwang, Essen.

convulsions. Their being was to shine like the roses in the windows of ancient cathedrals. The dark was to sink into pure light. One's own will, the personal, was to dissolve into the essential."[38]

And yet the Cabaret Voltaire was also the launch pad for the techniques that the Berlin Dadaists used to conjure the brutality of the present. Marcel Janco's masks, symbols of the standardized subjectivity of the modern metropolis (Figure 4);[39] the "noise music" of Huelsenbeck's drum, intended to drown out the noise of cannons;[40] the "Negro" or "simultaneous" poetry of Tristan Tzara, expressing a subjectivity that had renounced unity;[41] the frenetic group dances on the Voltaire stage:[42] these were all facets of a mimetic practice that apotropaically reorganized the givens of the contemporary world.[43] This was the direction taken by the Berlin Dadaists,[44] who stubbornly and almost exclusively replaced intercessors from distant cultures with ordinary objects from their own

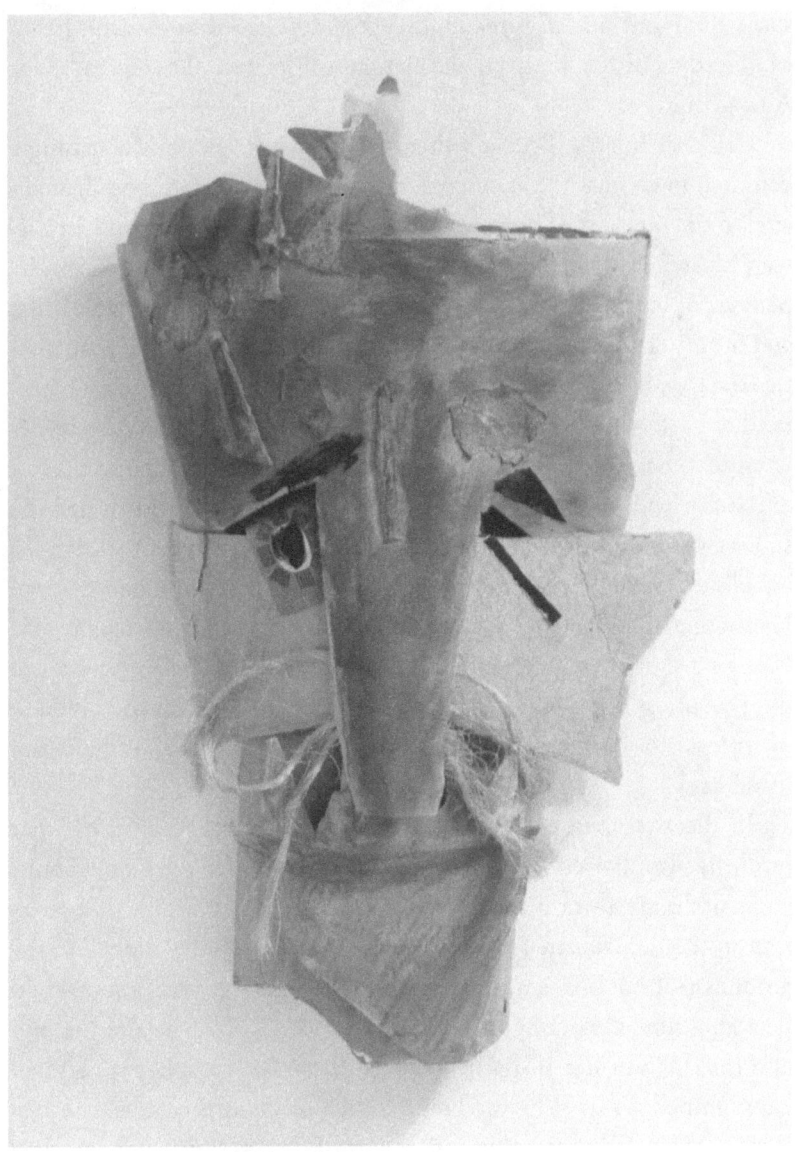

**FIGURE 4.** Marcel Janco, *Untitled* (*Mask*), 1919, paper, board, twine, gouache, and pastel, 45 × 22 × 5 cm (17 ¹¹⁄₁₆ × 8 ¹¹⁄₁₈ × 1 ¹⁵⁄₁₆ inches); Centre Pompidou, MNAM, gift of the artist, 1967. Source: Catalog Dada, National Gallery of Art, Washington, 2006. © ADAGP, Paris 2015.

space-time continuum. After all, these objects seemed to transmit forces as unsettling as the ancestral and natural spirits were thought to be for African cultures.

Criticism of the Brücke's literal primitivism became increasingly common in Germany, encouraging the emergence of a transposed, mediated, more open, and more exclusively functional primitivism.[45] In 1915 Carl Einstein interpreted *Negerplastik* as the alternative model chosen by painters of his time to escape the imitative ontology of their own culture and history. This kind of sculpture, through its arrangement of pure plastic relations, had a precise ontological function: it answered the subject's need to pacify the alterity of nature and the past, but without thereby devouring it. For Einstein, the lofty—because nonmimetic—transcendence of African sculpture and, inversely, African practices that identified the subject with an alterity mediated by masks, tattoos, and ritual dances, established a pact of nondevouring between man and his milieu.[46] Raoul Hausmann and Hannah Höch, as well as other Dadaists no doubt, read Einstein's short work attentively;[47] Einstein also took part in several of the Dadaist political editorials in Berlin.[48] His theories on the function of art in history coincided at that time perfectly with those of the Berlin Dadaists.

In the aftermath of World War I and the Spartacist uprising that immediately followed it, the Berlin Dadaists contested the Expressionist tactic of fleeing a world "full to the point of suffocation"[49] to find salvation in the immaculate space of the mind and art. They did so on the grounds that not only was salvation something that by definition would be a long time in coming, whether in this world or in the afterlife, but also that the war had just cruelly belied the apocalyptic hopes that had been pinned on it. Whereas Franz Marc's soliloquizing horses turned their backs to the spectator and Kandinsky's ethereal forms knocked against one another in the gravity-less space of Spirit, the objects of the contemporary world succeeded in contaminating men without their knowledge.[50] Humans had become as sterile, rigid, and fossilized as the very objects they were trying to flee. This is why it became urgent for the Dadaists to reverse the Expressionist strategy; to paraphrase Hugo Ball, what was most "incredible" in this "unnaturalness" turned out to be the unnaturalness itself.

We know that in the massive "return to objects" that took place in painting during the years after World War I, it was the strand of metaphysical painting that most appealed to German Dadaists. Despite its heavy symbolism, nostalgia, and nationalist assumptions, the defamiliarizing use of ordinary objects in the paintings of Giorgio de Chirico (Figure 5) and Carlo Carrà ultimately produced an incongruous temporality of great interest to the Dadaists. According to de Chirico, it was precisely because memory had deserted the world of things—the war had merely completed the process that he had already detected before 1914—that things were once again able to take on metaphysical meaning; it was because the world had reached its end that it could recommence its tertiary age, an age in which objects had not yet delivered their secrets to man.[51]

Historiography has neglected this macroscopic facet of Dadaist simultaneousness, which must be taken into account: the Dadaist present, a posthistory and prehistory at once, was formed from the vestiges of a civilization that in a sense did not yet exist. Hannah Höch's *Mechanical Garden* (1920; Figure 6) is a landscape unsuited to human beings, though it is composed of man-made fossils.[52] The geological cuts in Max Ernst's "overpaintings" (*Übermalereien*) also reveal fossilized specimens, though these had been created by the thousands in the factories of the past (Figure 7).[53] Both artists saw themselves as survivors and first men or women (*Urmensch*) at once and strove to show that they had inherited procedures and objects created by modern rationalization but had not yet found the means to control them. Their task was to learn the modes of mastering a dysfunctional reality and to train others in this "second prehistory."[54]

Several years later, on the eve of another war, Walter Benjamin explicitly attributed this function to the art of his time. In 1935, in the first version of his essay on the work of art, where he based his hypothesis of the

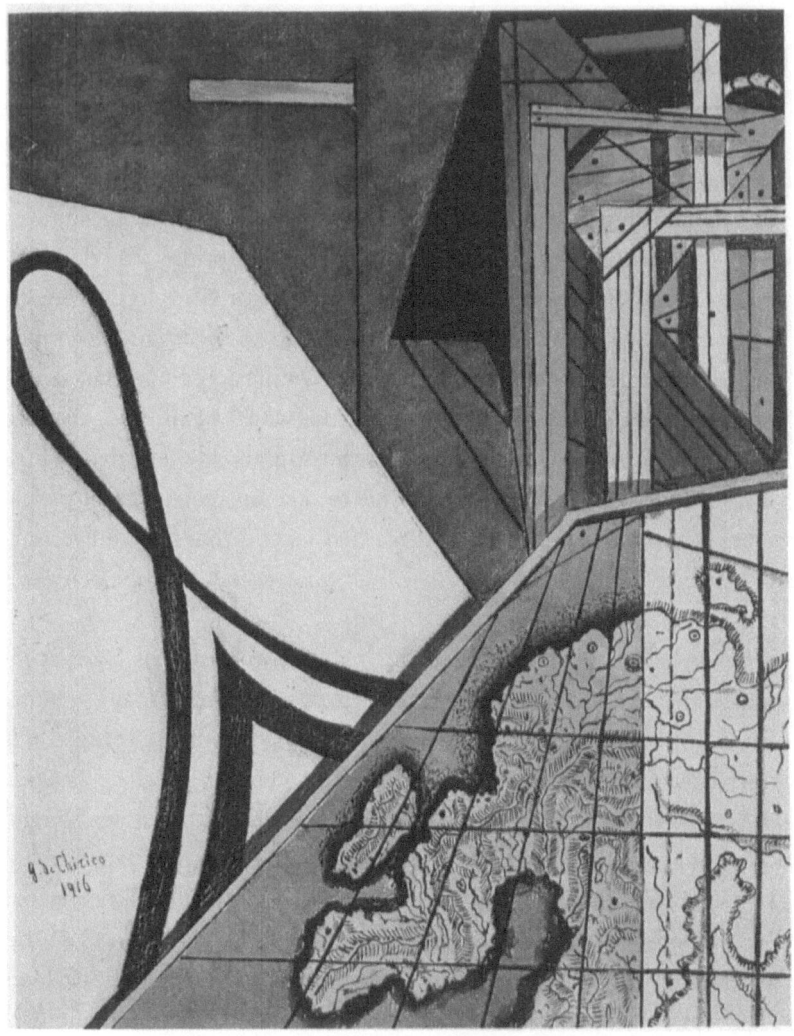

**FIGURE 5.** Giorgio de Chirico, *Melancholy of Departure*, 1916, oil on canvas, 51.8 × 36 cm; Tate Gallery, London. Source: Catalog Giergio de Chirico: la fabrique des rêves; Musée d'art moderne de la Ville de Paris, 2009. © ADAGP, Paris 2015.

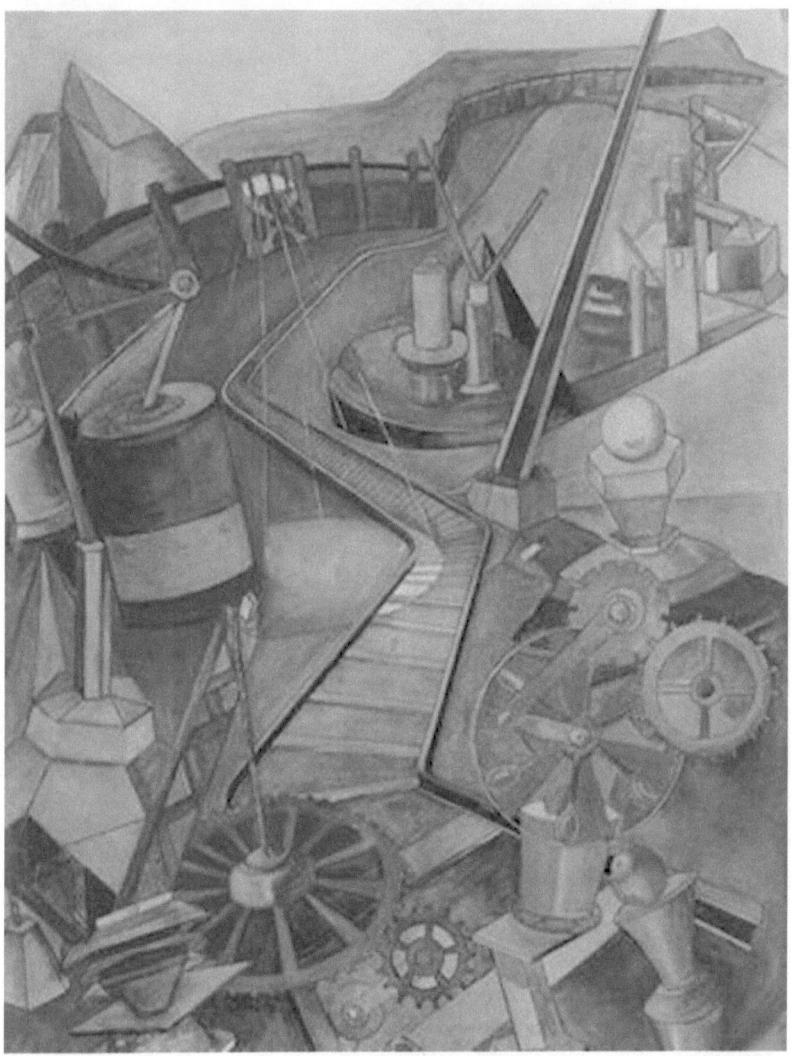

**FIGURE 6.** Hannah Höch, *Mechanical Garden* (*Mechanischer Garten*), 1920, gouache, aquarelle, pencil, and ink on paper, 73 × 47 cm (28 ³/₄ × 18 ¹/₂ inches); Christies Images Limited. Source: Cahiers du MNAM, 2009. © ADAGP, Paris 2015.

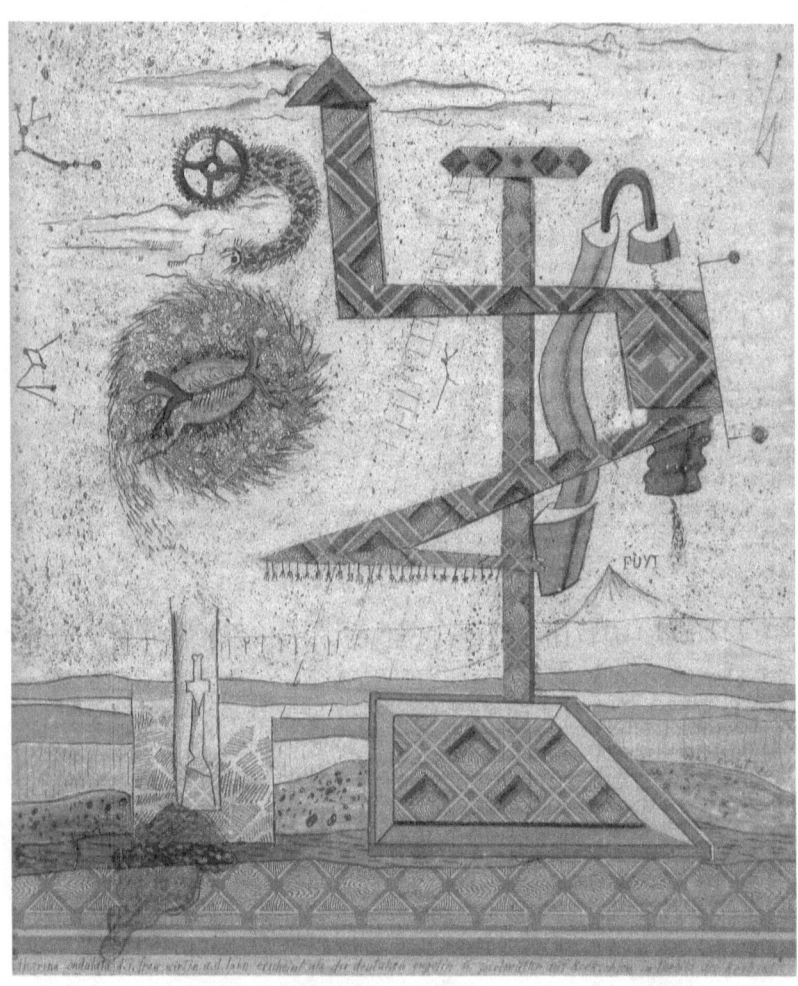

**FIGURE 7.** Max Ernst, *Katharina Ondulata*, 1920, gouache, pencil, and ink on printed paper, 31.5 × 27.5 cm; Scottish National Gallery of Modern Art, Edinburgh. Source: Werner Spies, Max Ernst. Les collages: inventaire et contradictions, Paris, Gallimard, 1984. © ADAGP, Paris 2015.

equivalence of prehistory and modernity on the increasing naturalization evident in modern technology that was freeing itself of man, he wrote:

> This emancipated technology stands across from today's society as a second nature, a nature no less elementary—as economic crises and wars prove—than that of primitive societies. Faced with this second nature, man, who invented it but who has long since ceased to be its master, is in need of training just like the one he needed when faced with the first nature. And once again, art provides this service.[55]

This is why Benjamin was so attentive to Dada, to the point of making it a concrete, though in his eyes insufficient, example of the materialist turn he advocated in art. Paradoxically, he recognized a prehistorical freeze in Dadaist works. The Dadaists put their finger on the problem: the need for art to create a new "use value" for itself, one that would be mediated by unknown forms of creation and reception—those very forms Carl Einstein evoked in his treatise *Negerplastik*, with the ultimate motive of extracting the modern subject from the illusion of his or her autonomous sphere.[56] Raoul Hausmann formulated this idea clearly.

> Man was art's most important subject, and as his optical capacities developed, the entire visible world became his conquest and art ceased to be a magical conjuration in the face of a disquieting reality. Reality was captured, appropriated, and tamed through representation, and art became nothing more than a game, a luxury, and thereby, a class privilege.[57]

However, the taming of a disquieting reality required that artists free themselves from the mediation of African artifacts, for the simple reason that a host of other objects capable of *magically conjuring* the present were at hand: "By presenting marionette life, mechanized life; by presenting real and apparent rigidification, [such objects] allow us to perceive and feel another kind of life."[58] Thus, whereas the Expressionists proclaimed the birth of a new man out of the ashes of the old, the Dadaists were interested in the inanimate state, which, according to Sigmund Freud in 1920, was not only the end but also the origin of life.[59]

This is more or less what Hausmann also believed. He wrote in a letter that it must never be forgotten that "life" is "woven of death": "The
will to adapt to what is foreign, to death, is balanced by the will to personality, to uniqueness, to life."[60] In other words, the Dadaists' apotropaic
mimetic strategy consisted in feigning death to remain alive, in imitating
the rigidity of the reified world to have some chance of discovering the
transformative power of subjectivity.[61] This paradoxical logic—which is a
general feature of mimesis but which Dadaism's vertiginous mix of death
drive and *élan vital* intensified—corresponded exactly to the movement's
temporal ambiguity.

In short, the Dadaist conception of transition was spatial as well as
temporal, but it was simultaneous rather than successive. It was a transition that was concentrated in the present. As Hausmann put it, "We
are hovering between two worlds; we have broken with the old world
before the new one has been formed, and satire, caricature, the grotesque, clownishness, and puppetry take the stage."[62] In the objects that
lay in the space between two worlds—the world of men and the world
of things, the world of life and the world of death—the Dadaists found
what was grotesque and satirical in their time.

# THE PRESENT AS REPRODUCIBLE TIME

## Not Document but Device

The photograph in Figure 8 has been reproduced dozens of times in works on the historical avant-garde movements in general and on Dada in particular. It is the indexical sign of a legendary event of which few traces remain today. The Erste Internationale Dada Messe, which took place in Berlin in the summer of 1920, has been interpreted variously as the height of Dadaist disobedience toward the public, institutions of art, and the authority of the state and the Communist Party; an amplification of the movement's destructive practices, which came tumbling out of individual works to fill the entire exhibit space; and finally, Dada's spectacular exit from the Berlin art scene of the 1920s.[1] But this photograph of the core members of Berlin Dada can also be understood on its own terms—that is, not as the transparent document of a legendary event but as a somewhat more opaque device, a meticulous staging of the formal, rhetorical, and ontological strategies forged by Dadaist subjectivity in its struggle with the temporality of the present. In the aftermath of a disastrous war, as the Spartacist revolution was tearing German society apart, these artists realized that mastering the present—by definition fleeting and more threatening than ever—meant defending its sovereignty

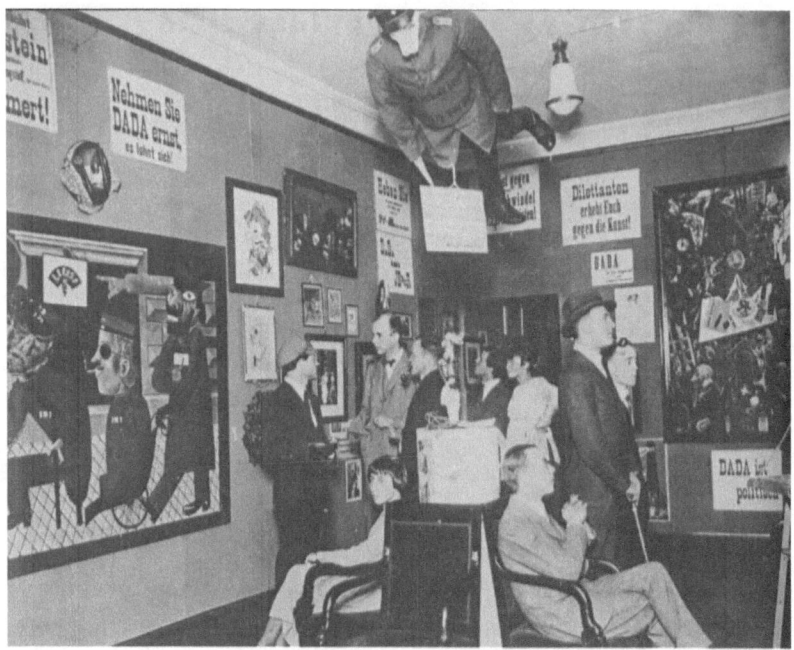

**FIGURE 8.** Opening of the First International Dada Fair (Erste Internationale Dada Messe), 1920. Source: Photograph originally published in Richard Huelsenbeck, *Dada Almanach*, Berlin, 1920.

against the normativity of the past and the utopia of the future, the two temporal orders that had confiscated the history of modern times.

The photograph in Figure 8 shows a divide. A line separates improvisation from pose, distraction from contemplation. A virtual medial axis runs through the space represented, from the pedestal on which there sits a small Max Ernst sculpture (*Phallustrade*, now lost), up to the famous mannequin of a policeman with the face of a pig hanging from the ceiling. The mannequin hovers at the peak of an optical pyramid and most certainly alludes to police surveillance in Germany, which intensified during the war, targeting society as a whole and artists in particular. The same symbolism, simple and direct in its logic, can be found, though inverted, in George Grosz's painting *Germany, A Winter's Tale* (1918, now lost) (Figure 9), also exhibited at the Dada Messe. The bourgeois man

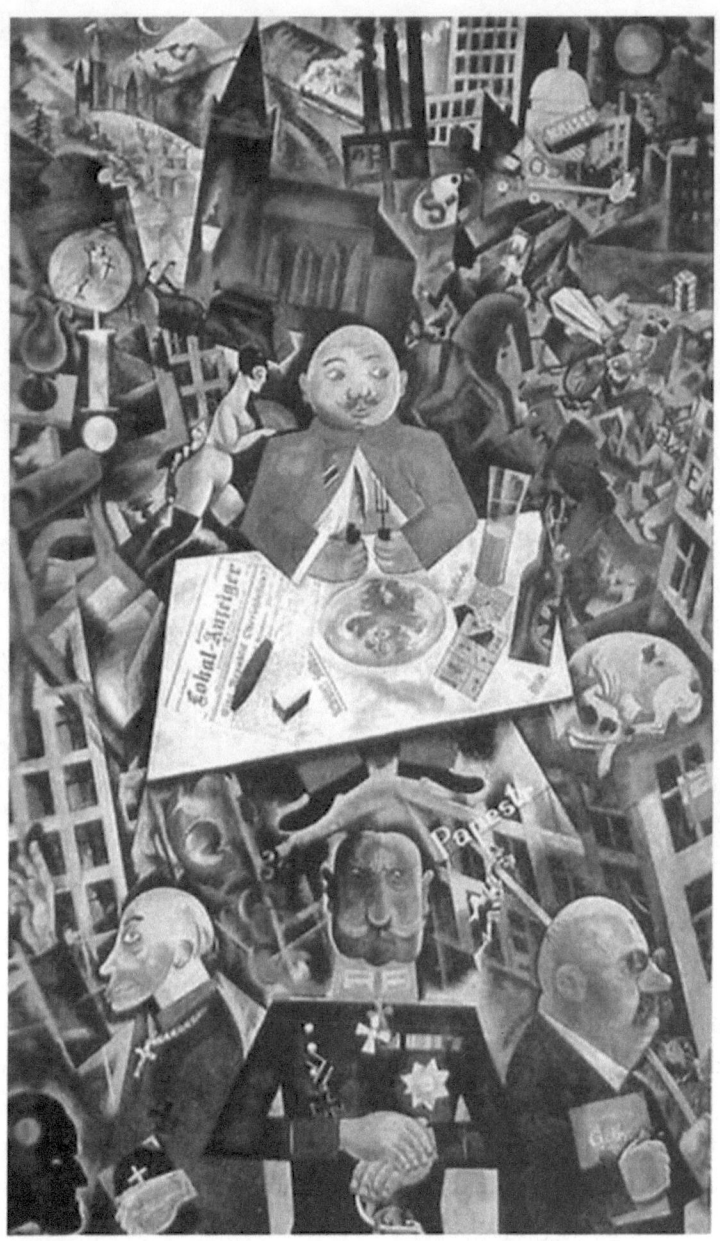

**FIGURE 9.** George Grosz, *Germany, A Winter's Tale*, 1918, oil on canvas (destroyed). © The Estate of George Grosz, Princeton, N.J. / ADAGP, Paris 2015.

sitting at the center of the composition is supported by the three pillars of church, state, and army.

A more subtle symbolism can be seen at the base of the photograph's optical pyramid, which is made up of the Dadaists themselves (see Figure 8). The left side of the photo is the side of instantaneity and captures a moment in which Raoul Hausmann, Johannes Baader, and the gallery owner, Otto Burchard, are conversing peacefully, their backs to the works on the wall behind them. On this same side, but further away and in the foreground, Hannah Höch is seated alone. A liminal figure, Höch turns her gaze out of the photograph's frame, looking in the opposite direction from the circle of three men, as though this detached, marginal position were a comment on her ex-centric and uncertain role as the sole woman of the group.[2] The figure of Otto Schmalhausen, on the right side of the photograph, is symmetric with Höch's; he is shown seated, hands crossed and arms laid on the armrests of his chair. Unlike Höch, his gaze is not ex-centric but rather directed toward the assemblage *The Middle-Class Philistine Heartfield Gone Wild* (1920, also lost).[3] Schmalhausen's gaze converges with that of the assemblage's two creators, George Grosz and John Heartfield, who stand stiffly at his side. Unlike the three men chatting across the room, Schmalhausen, Grosz, and Heartfield show no relation to one another. Their proximity seems random and arbitrary, entirely unmotivated. Each is riveted to himself, absorbed in intimate contemplation of the out-of-frame assemblage atop its improvised pedestal. But these postures and the spatial arrangement of the photograph as a whole—which activates themes of contemplation and distraction, rigid and relaxed poses, the individual and the collective—function too well together to have been mere coincidence. The snapshot seems to dissimulate the time that must have been spent on preliminary formal elaboration—that is, the time span of the work necessary to effectively defend the sovereignty of the present instant.

### Grosz and Heartfield:
### Counter-Gap as Strategy for Actualizing the Past

The main component of the "electro-mechanic sculpture" in which Schmalhausen, Grosz, and Heartfield are absorbed is a tailor's mannequin (Figure 10). A prosthesis fills in for his missing leg, and he has a lit light bulb for a head. From a purely iconological point of view, the disparate objects attached to his chest evoke the whole closed world of the petit bourgeois: the doorbell evokes his protective house; two broken pieces of silverware allude to the uninterrupted cycle of biological preservation; a pistol and medal testify to his recent exploits during the war; and the number 27 indicates the reproducibility of this anonymous subject in the world of modern rationalization. As the dentures he has in place of genitals testify, the petit bourgeois John Heartfield has repressed his drives—all but the drive to kill, to which the military insignia he wears testifies, as does, by antiphrasis, his own prosthesis.

That prosthesis contains the full critical force of the two artists' maneuver in relation to history, both ancient and contemporary. It is used here as a means of actualizing the past and aims at both the devaluation of a certain nineteenth-century understanding of history—in particular, historicism and the normativity of antiquity—and a materialist affirmation of the present. It is thus the complex, though hardly contradictory, sign of the depreciation of the antiquarian spirit and the defense of a certain historical materialism. Potentially ambiguous, the prosthesis thus exceeds the hermeneutic resources of iconology and only becomes fully intelligible as the centerpiece of a critical montage.

Jean-Claude Lebensztejn explains that neoclassicism postulates a counter-gap that fills in the initial distance separating nature from art, the particular from the universal, the senses from reason, and matter from ideal.[4] The Dadaist mannequin's prosthesis turns this counter-gap on itself, thus undermining neoclassicism's untimely norm from within. A literal corrective to nature, a remedy for the accidents to which life, unlike Spirit, is subjected, the Dadaist prosthesis turns the assemblage into a

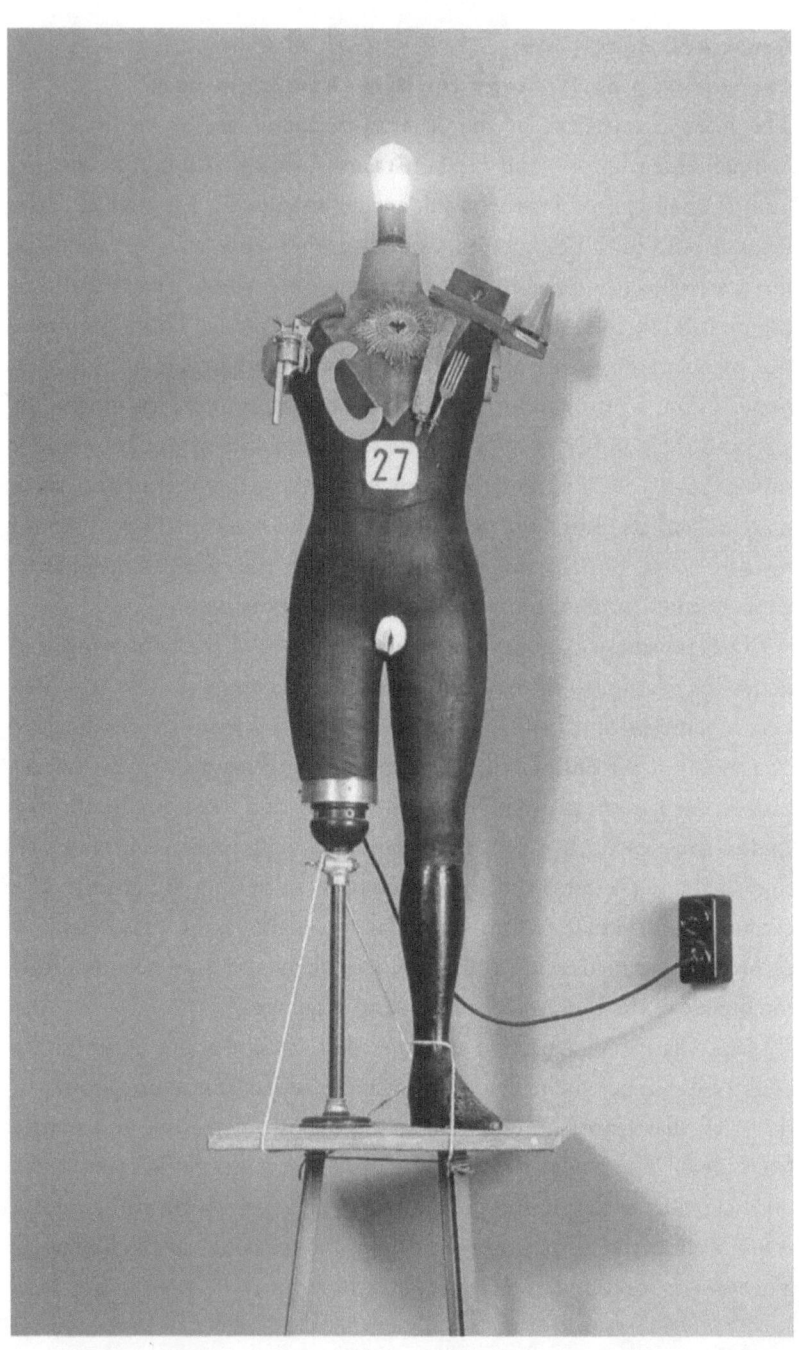

sign with two different aspects and two distinct temporalities: on the one hand, the temporality of an ancient sculpture, torn out of the denseness of time and partly spared its ravages, displayed on a pedestal in a museum space; on the other hand, the temporality of an imperial soldier recently converted into a worker for the brand-new republic. "The wearer of the prosthesis is . . . a man of the highest quality, raised, so to speak, to a new rank thanks to the world war,"[5] Hausmann wrote in one of his satires fustigating the ergonomic ideology applied to war invalids.[6] The Dadaists were acutely aware of the incongruous connections between techniques of spiritual and moral elevation and techniques of material production. The assemblage's reference to the policy of recycling the workforce and its remnants—from behind the lines to the front and back again— extended beyond the limits of the work into the space of the exhibition; the assemblage stood in dialogue with the Otto Dix painting across from it, *45% Erwerbsfähig* ("45% Able to Work"; destroyed), depicting a grotesque procession of the war's wounded (see Figure 8).[7]

The semiotic and temporal ambivalence found in Grosz and Heartfield's assemblage—between Spirit and matter, between the nobility of antiquity and the brutality of the present—becomes even clearer in comparison with Rudolf Schlichter's more rudimentary montage of past and present in his work *Corrected Masterpieces*, also on display at the Dada Messe. By placing banal heads atop copies of the Venus de Milo and the Belvedere Apollo, Schlichter intended to show that in the age of mechanical reproducibility, the ideal—that norm that looms behind every artwork—had become standardized kitsch.[8] Despite the qualitative

**FIGURE 10.** (*opposite*) George Grosz and John Heartfield, *The Middle-Class Philistine Heartfield Gone Wild (Electro-Mechanical Tatlin Sculpture)* (Der wildgewordene Spiesser Heartfield [Electro-mechan. Tatlin-Plastik]), 1988 (reconstruction of 1920 original), tailor's dummy, revolver, doorbell, knife, fork, letter C and number 27 signs, plaster dentures, embroidered insignia for the Black Eagle Order on horse blanket, Osram light bulb, Iron Cross, stand, and other objects, 220 × 45 × 45 cm (85 $^{13}\!/_{16}$ × 17 $^{11}\!/_{16}$ × 17 $^{11}\!/_{18}$ inches); Berlinische Galerie, Berlin. Source: Catalog Dada, National Gallery of Art, Washington, 2006 © The estate of George Grosz, Princeton, N.J. / ADAGP, Paris 2015. © The Heartfield Community of Heirs / ADAGP, Paris 2015.

differences between their respective rhetorical strategies, the three Dadaists' references to antiquity—literal in Schlichter's work, metaphorical in
Grosz and Heartfield's—shared a common principle that we might call
actualization of the past.[9]

This principle was outlined by Wieland Herzfelde, editor at the
Malik Verlag and brother of John Heartfield, in his text for the Dada
Messe catalog.

> The past remains important and authoritative only to the extent that
> its cult must be combated. The Dadaists are of one mind: they say
> that the works of antiquity, the classical age, and all the "great minds"
> must not be evaluated (unless in a scientifically historical manner) with
> regard to the age in which they were created, but as if someone made
> those things today.[10]

What did Herzfelde mean by this? That the Dada artists were invert-
ing the play of historical forces by subjecting the past to what it itself had
subjected nature and successive presents to over the course of centuries.
Through their process of actualization, they wanted to show that the past
was entirely unsuited to the present and displayed an absolute anach-
ronism. As for the Dadaists themselves, they revealed an acute sense of
historical relativism, which—at least since Herder—has recognized a temporality proper to even the smallest historical trace.[11] They observed that
the past had had a long life and had, in a sense, profited from what we
might call an *absolute temporal plus-value.* The Dadaist strategy consisted
in treating this plus-value as follows: by bringing the absolute past onto
the slippery plank of the present, they intended quite simply to show its
inadequacy. In so doing, the Dadaists distanced themselves from another
scorner of the antiquarian spirit, one on whom they had, however, drawn
in their parody of history. By using what was most banal in their own
time to devalue the past, the Dadaists inverted the Nietzschean imperative
to monumentalize the present on the basis of great examples from history, which inspired many early twentieth-century reforms in Germany.[12]
Their "present interest"[13] and their faith in the utility of forgetting di-

verged considerably from Nietzsche's in his second "untimely meditation." As we will see, some Dadaists practiced such radical forgetting that
they transformed life into eternal becoming.[14] For this reason, although
the Dadaists were powerful actualizations of Baudelaire's painter of modern life—who was "a kaleidoscope gifted with consciousness," an "'I' with
an insatiable appetite for the 'non-I'"—they shattered the duality that the
Romantic poet established between "an eternal, invariable element" and
"a relative, circumstantial element, which will be, if you like, whether sev-
erally or all at once, the age, its fashions, its morals, its emotions."[15]

The Dadaist as ahistorical (*unhistorisch*), as a mirror indifferently
capturing the flow of images passing by without retaining any, is one of
the structural figures of Dadaist discourse on subjectivity. But the idea
of the vital utility of radically forgetting the past is also something the
Dadaists owed to the Futurists, the first avant-garde movement to have
clearly expressed the conversion of mourning for a lost object—God,
the glorious national past, an effective collective art—into the maniacal
creation of something new.

Éric Michaud found in Freud's analysis of mourning—which postulates that melancholy turns into mania—a conceptual device that strongly
shaped the inaugural moment of modern art, Romanticism, oscillating
between threat and consolation.[16] Unsurprisingly, this conceptual device
found striking currency in the offensive practices of avant-garde movements, from Futurism to Picasso in the *Demoiselles d'Avignon* and the
threatening *Dryad*, or to Duchamp, who in 1912 decided to no longer be
"the sad man in a train."[17] Filippo Marinetti explained the Futurist project as the transformation of a latecomer's inhibiting pessimism into the
"artificial optimism" of forerunners.[18] Fortunato Depero and Giacomo
Balla incorporated Marinetti's words into their manifesto on the "plastic complex" (Figure II), the Futurist name for assemblage, which they
conceived of as an artificial, polysensory "organism" and which was the
culmination of the Darwinist evolution of man and art.

> Before us, art relied on memory, an anxious re-evocation of an Object lost
> (happiness, love, a landscape), and hence was nostalgic, static, charged

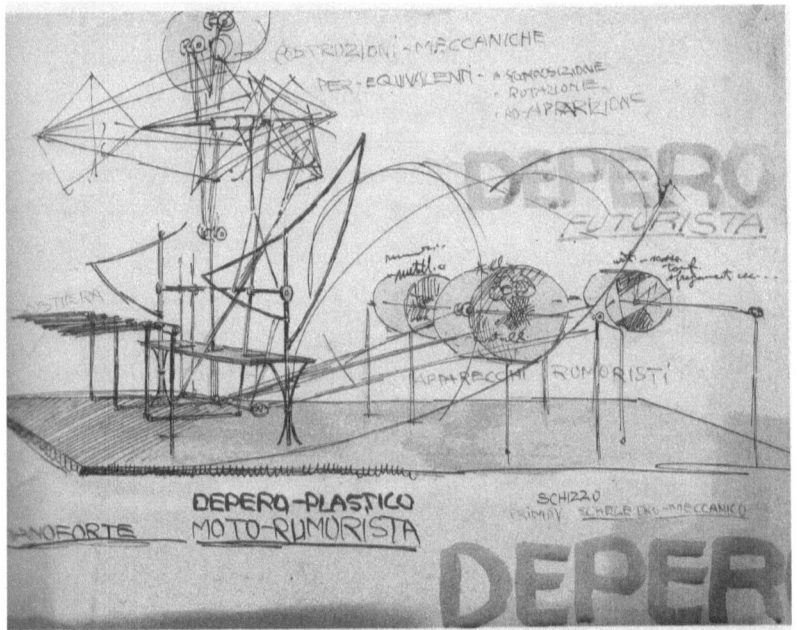

**FIGURE 11.** Fortunato Depero, *Compresso plastico motorumorista a luminosità colorate e spruzzatore*, c. 1915, ink on paper, 16 × 17 cm; Museo di arte moderna e contemporanea di Trento e Rovereto (Arhivio Fotographico e Medieteca Mart). Source: Museo di arte moderna e contemporanea di Trento e Rovereto. © ADAGP, Paris 2015.

with suffering and distance. With Futurism, instead, art is turning into art-action, which is to say, into will, optimism, aggression, possession, penetration, delight, brutal reality within art (example: onomatopoeia;— example: noise-tuners = motors), geometrical splendor of forces, projections forward. Thus, art is becoming Presence, new Object, new reality created with the abstract elements of the universe. The hands of the passéist artist used to suffer for the sake of the lost Object; our hand will twitch for the new Object to be created. That is why the new Object (the plastic complex) has miraculously appeared in your hands.[19]

The "new object" was the direct product of these artists' decision to stop sacrificing their art to the rapacity of memory, to stop paying homage to painting, which, at least since Alberti, has been understood as the presentification of absence or the resurrection of the dead. Herzfelde, in his text on the Dada Messe, used the same argument, but as a resolute Marxist, he replaced the Futurists' moral, atemporal values—will, optimism, action, aggression, possession—with the effects that the means of production of his time had on art and its temporal orders.

> Painting once had the explicit aim of providing people with a view of things—landscapes, animals, buildings, and so forth—that they could not come to know with their own eyes. Today this task has been taken over by photography and film, which accomplish it incomparably better and more completely than painters of any era.
>
> Yet painting did not die with the loss of its objective, but instead sought new ones. Since then, all aspirations to art, no matter how various they may be, can be grouped together insofar as they have in common a tendency to emancipate themselves from reality.
>
> Dadaism is the reaction against all those attempts to disavow the actual that were the driving force of the Impressionists, Expressionists, Cubists, and Futurists.[20]

Abstraction and the various isms were thus considered techniques of repression created by painters confronted with the decreasing value of their art as a result of mechanical reproducibility. The reason for this was not just that painting could no longer be *reproductive*, because this function had been taken over by intrinsically *reproducible* media. It was also that art in general had to end its practice of spatiotemporal *trans*position, its detours through the lost object—which were still practiced by Expressionism and abstraction—in favor of an ideology of direct, immediate presence and expression.[21] However, for the Dadaists, there was nothing unique or irreplaceable about this presence, and it lacked the warmth of human breath. According to Herzfelde, the only "hic et nunc" available was the product of an impassive machine. As such, it was available by the thousands.

> The Dadaists say: When in the past colossal quantities of time, love, and effort were directed toward the painting of a body, a flower, a hat, a

heavy shadow, and so forth, now we need merely to take scissors and cut out all that we require from paintings and photographic representations of these things; when something on a smaller scale is involved, we do not need representations at all but take instead the objects themselves, for example, pocketknives, ashtrays, books, etc., all things that, in the museums of old art, have been painted very beautifully indeed, but have been, nonetheless, merely painted.[22]

By renouncing painting as transposition, Dadaist art also switched temporal regimes: through the reproducibility and presence it proclaimed for itself, it allowed itself to be absorbed by the flow of time. Dadaist photomontages, assemblages, actions, and proclamations not only drew their themes from the present but also physically participated in it. John Heartfield (that is, Helmut Herzfeld) explained this process of literalization to Count Harry Kessler, who wrote about it with perspicacity in his journal.

> A visit from Helmut Herzfeld. In connection with his periodical, he expressed his utter repugnance to the publication of poems by Däubler or Becher or indeed anything that is just art. He and his friends, he explained, are becoming more and more hostile to art. Wieland's and George Grosz's achievements are, it is true, artistic, but only so to speak as a by-product. The main thing is to echo the heart-beat of our days. He went on to reject past artistic achievement too, even if in its own time it did possess precisely this quality of contemporaneity. He and his friends do not want either to document their actions or to create any kind of durable record and thus to impede posterity.[23]

The Dadaists' understanding of art was thus impervious to the distinction between monument and document that Erwin Panofsky later formulated in his reflections on method in history.[24] They contested the humanist postulate that distinguished the object of historical study from its instrument. They did not recognize the traditional form of history, which, as Michel Foucault put it in *The Archaeology of Knowledge*, "undertook to 'memorize' the *monuments* of the past, transform them into *documents*, and lend speech to those traces which, in themselves, are often not verbal, or which say in silence something other than what they actually say."[25] This is why they deliberately engaged with the documentary status of photography, an essential component of the medium. Aware of the semantic potential of the documentary nature of photography for history, they simply diverted that potential, not to leave it behind but to formulate their own conception of history and art.

It should be noted that the history defended by most Dadaists was not at all Foucauldian, in that it never abandoned its ultimate unity and meaning, which it attributed to the right correlation of present and future. This was true, in any case, for the Marxist trio made up of Grosz and the Herzfelde brothers (we will see that there were multiple uses of history in Dadaism). Discerning and defending the meaning of history ultimately meant splitting history as a "singular collective," as Reinhart Koselleck described it, into two: by refusing to grant their works the status of virtual documents of the past to be used by the future, the Dadaists expressed their rejection of traditional history (*Historie*), fossilized in its documents, so as to better defend another kind of history (*Geschichte*), a history that could be made by man, because it is active in itself from the beginning. This is also why the photograph of the Dada Messe (Figure 8) was less an event torn from the continuum of passing time and more a formal construction—a device—signaling the times to come.[26]

### The Temporalization of Art:
### Historicism and Reproducibility

In his 1921 text on Dada, Roman Jakobson noted a double paradox created by modern art's continuous transgression of the past: the "legalization of illegality" and the devaluation of successive artistic currents.[27] Although Futurism understood this double paradox, it could not deduce all its consequences; on the contrary, Futurism passionately aspired to become classical by establishing itself over time. Jakobson's critique was perspicacious; the paintings of Umberto Boccioni, for example, express the struggle between the artist's will to constitute himself as the solid core of his composition—his quasidivine control over the world in its simultaneity—and his desire to empathically identify with the dissolving simultaneity of things. The same double bind can be seen in the way the bodies of his sculptures are anchored in their bases, signaling a sovereign autonomy. Boccioni sought, however, to combat through the plastic fusion of that body with the world around it (Figure 12).[28]

Whereas Futurism failed to escape these contradictions, Jakobson found that Dada triumphed over all involuntary logical contradictions. He saw Dada as the artistic correlate to Albert Einstein's theories in science, Nikolai Bukharin's in economics, and Oswald Spengler's in history, for all four shared an acute sense of relativity. Things had no absolute value in time or space not only because they were ephemeral but also because their interdependence far exceeded their individual particularities. According to Jakobson, the "great historian" Spengler (who, as we know, had a major impact on Russia's most progressive circles[29]) had even proven "the impossibility of history as a science."[30] Jakobson was convinced that Dada could have recognized itself in this conclusion. The linguist was wrong about this, but he was right, of course, to see in Dadaism a rigorous defense of the temporalization of history. As we have seen, this temporalization was also required by the reproducible materials of photography as well as film, one of the structural models of Dadaist subjectivity and artworks.[31]

But it is Siegfried Kracauer and his writings connecting history and photography who, even more than Spengler, can help us understand Dadaism's temporalities and its conception of history, even if Kracauer's "unhappy consciousness" during these years stood in stark contrast to the ontological postulates of the Dada artists. In his 1927 essay on photography, Kracauer pointed out the structural analogy between that medium and historicism.

> [Both] think that they can explain any phenomenon purely in terms of its genesis. That is, they believe at the very least that they can grasp historical reality by reconstructing the series of events in their temporal

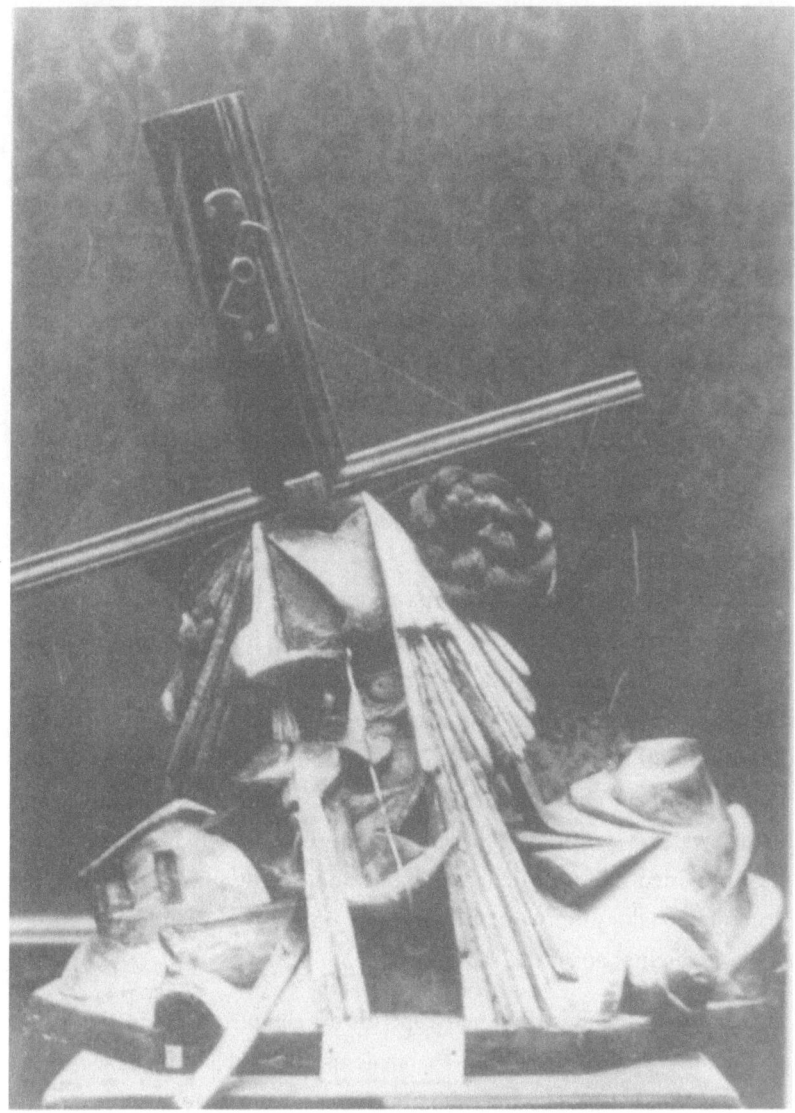

**FIGURE 12.** Umberto Boccioni, *Fusion of a Head and a Window* (*Fusione di una testa e di une finestra*), c. 1912 (later destroyed); photograph by Luca Carrà, Milan; Courtesy Angelo Calmarini, Milan.Ester Cohen, Umberto Boccioni, The MET, NY, 1988. © Studio Fotografico Luca Carrà.

succession without any gaps. Photography presents a spatial continuum; historicism seeks to provide the temporal continuum.[32]

Historicism meant that the historian's task was to show "what actually happened" (*wie es eigentlich gewesen*) to use Leopold von Ranke's famous phrase;[33] this would yield the infallible, unequivocal, deducible chain of causes and effects to which history could be reduced. As for photography, as Herzfelde saw, the topos that marked photographic invention above all was that of exalting or deploring its incomparable realism, inherent in its status as indexical sign. Thus both historicism and photography claimed a quasigenetic relationship to their objects, which Kracauer ultimately interpreted as the source of their all-consuming attitude toward time and space: global history sought to incorporate the totality of events into its narrative; photographic ubiquity was capable of recording the totality of things.

Kracauer's 1927 essay—the first moment in his sustained examination of the relations between photography and history—found one of its most faithful heirs in Susan Sontag, who, at the end of the 1970s, also interpreted photography's "passivity" and "ubiquity" as the two qualities determining the medium's drive to devour and its consequent fetishizing usage of history.[34] For Kracauer, the bulimic nature of photography and history was the symptom of a denial of finitude, of which the illustrated press provided the most delirious expression. In the illustrated press, the structural analogy between history and photography collapsed into a single, indistinct entity.

> The aim of the illustrated newspapers is the complete reproduction of the world accessible to the photographic apparatus; they record the spatial outlines of people, conditions, and events from every possible perspective. . . . Never before has an age been so informed about itself, if being informed means having an image of objects that resembles them in a photographic sense. . . . But the flood of photos sweeps away the dams of memory. The assault of this mass of images is so powerful that it threatens to destroy the potentially existing awareness of crucial traits.[35]

Like Kracauer, the Dadaists saw that the illustrated press was both the expression and the tool of the regime of simultaneity in effect in the world. Day after day, around the world, photographic journalism captured people and events as they really were. But whereas Kracauer intended to protect consciousness by reinforcing the dams separating it from the flood of corrupting images, Dadaist mimesis used the illustrated press as one of its favorite materials.[36] Thus Hannah Höch wrote the history of her time using documents drawn from the daily illustrated newspaper *BIZ* (*Berlinische Illustrierte Zeitung*). She dug her "kitchen knife" into the "beer-filled belly of the Weimar Republic," where, gathered in disorder, were men and things, the solemn and the banal, the president of the republic and his minister of the interior in official uniform or in bathing suits, Albert Einstein and some famous dancer, and finally, the Dadaists themselves, rubbing shoulders with the impurity of their time and willingly adopting its entirely relative values (Figure 13).[37] The goal was not simply to exalt the relativity intrinsic to modern times but to make clear that this relativity was really a co-relativity.

### Johannes Baader:
### The End of Mourning and the
### Artist's Transformation into Eternal Present

In truth, the only Dadaist to have adopted an absolute—and thereby dead-end—relativism was Johannes Baader. No other Dadaist explored the ambiguous relations between history and the press as systematically and unsettlingly as he did. It is as though, through a process of neutralization, his own madness helped him rationally pierce the madness of his time. This of course presupposes that Baader added a third term to the relation between press and history: the autobiographical element, the real and fictional history of his own person.

Baader's legendary yet ephemeral work *Plasto-Dio-Dada-Drama: Germany's Greatness and Decline* (1920, now lost) was at the center of the second Dada Messe exhibit room. Only two photographs of the work remain today (Figures 14 and 15). It was a five-level construction placed on a table

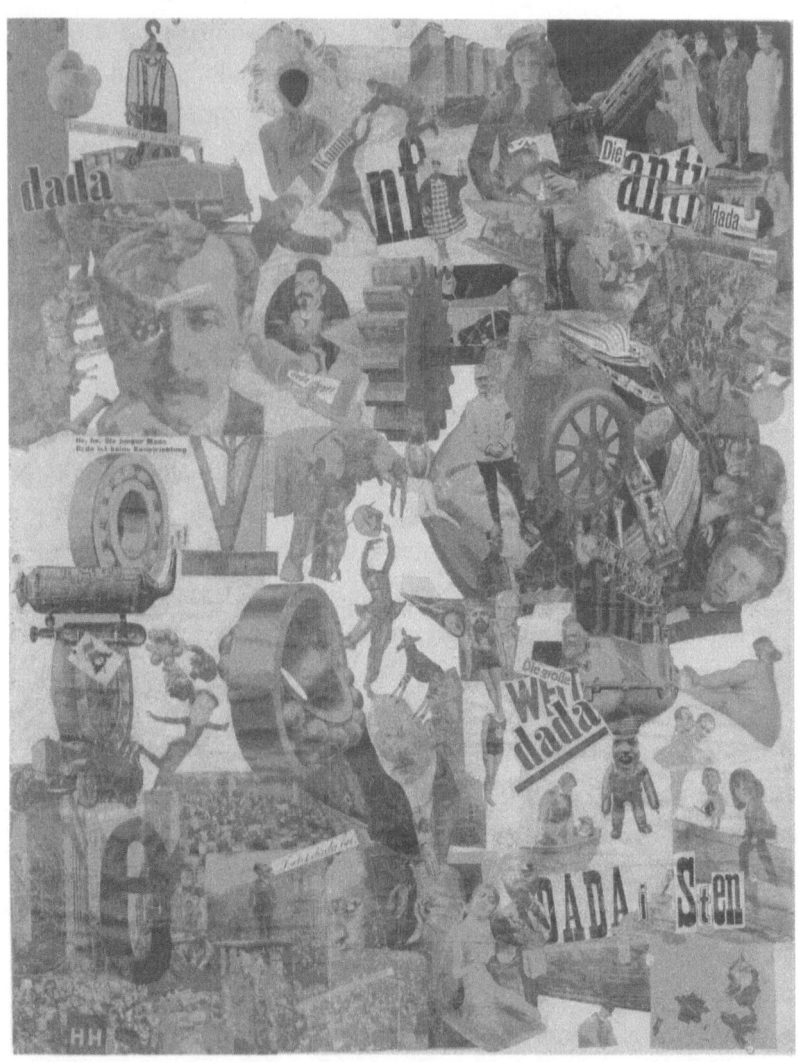

**FIGURE 13.** Hannah Höch, *Schnitt mit dem Küchenmesser Dada durch die letzte Weimarer Bierbauchkulturepoche Deutschlands* (*Cut with the Kitchen Knife Dada Through the Last Weimar Beer-Belly Cultural Epoch in Germany*), 1919–1920, photomontage and collage with watercolor on paper, 114 × 90 cm (44 ⅞ × 36 ½₆ inches); Staatliche Museen zu Berlin, Nationalgalerie. Source: Catalog Dada, National Gallery of Art, Washington, 2006. © ADAGP, Paris 2015.

covered with a large sheet of paper on which were glued pages with Dadaist phonetic poems (Hausmann's in particular) printed on them. Because of the assemblage's fragmented composition, it is impossible to immediately distinguish the five floors in the photographs. They were made out of papers hung on an invisible structure; the papers came from Baader's personal archives, the contemporary press, and Dadaist publications (*Die freie Strasse, Die Pleite,* etc.). Complete objects as well as fragments were added to this: pipes of all sorts, wheels, and machine parts—objects used for passage, circulation, connection. In other words, these objects utterly lacked self-sufficiency. Finally, a male mannequin was placed next to the assemblage. It would later reappear in Baader's work (the circulation of motifs between works of the same or different artists was another hallmark of the Dada network).[38] The mannequin was dressed in formal attire, and his painted head, with impeccably combed hair, lowered gaze, and mustached smile, gave him a docile and reserved air.

Baader interpreted his strange construction in a text published shortly after the Dada Messe by Richard Huelsenbeck in *The Dada Almanach.*[39] Pushing symbolism to the point of absurdity, Baader provided a great deal of detail about the meaning of his work, constantly changing register and going from universal history to the history of the Empire, from his own autobiography and personal production to art history of all ages, from declinism to messianism, and from the hyperbole of legend to the "factuality" of journalistic documents. Drawing on a long German intellectual tradition, Baader explored the analogy between his own personal bildungsroman and the nation's: "Preparation, Metaphysical Test, Inauguration, World War, World Revolution" were the five decisive stages of these two stories.

Adrian Sudhalter, in her invaluable work on Baader, notes that Baader's birth (1875) and the founding of the empire (1871) were practically contemporaneous.[40] Thus it was not difficult for the artist to place the site where the two destinies were being prepared in the foundation of the assemblage, which, covered with paper, was hidden from sight. A bit higher up in *Plasto-Dio-Dada-Drama,* the birth of the artist coincided with the founding of the empire. Next, a "panorama of culture"

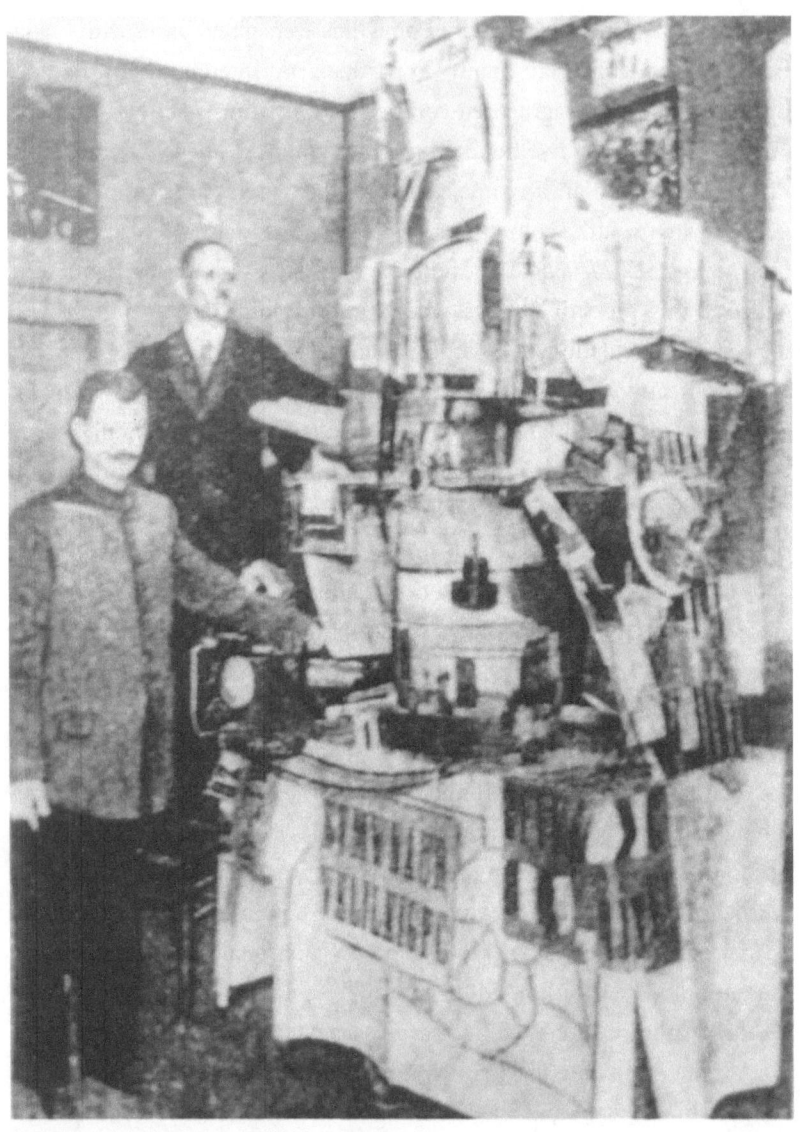

**FIGURE 14.** Photograph of Johannes Baader's *Great Plasto-Dio-Dada-Drama*, with Baader seen at left. Source: Tillburgsche Courant, VI, 1920.

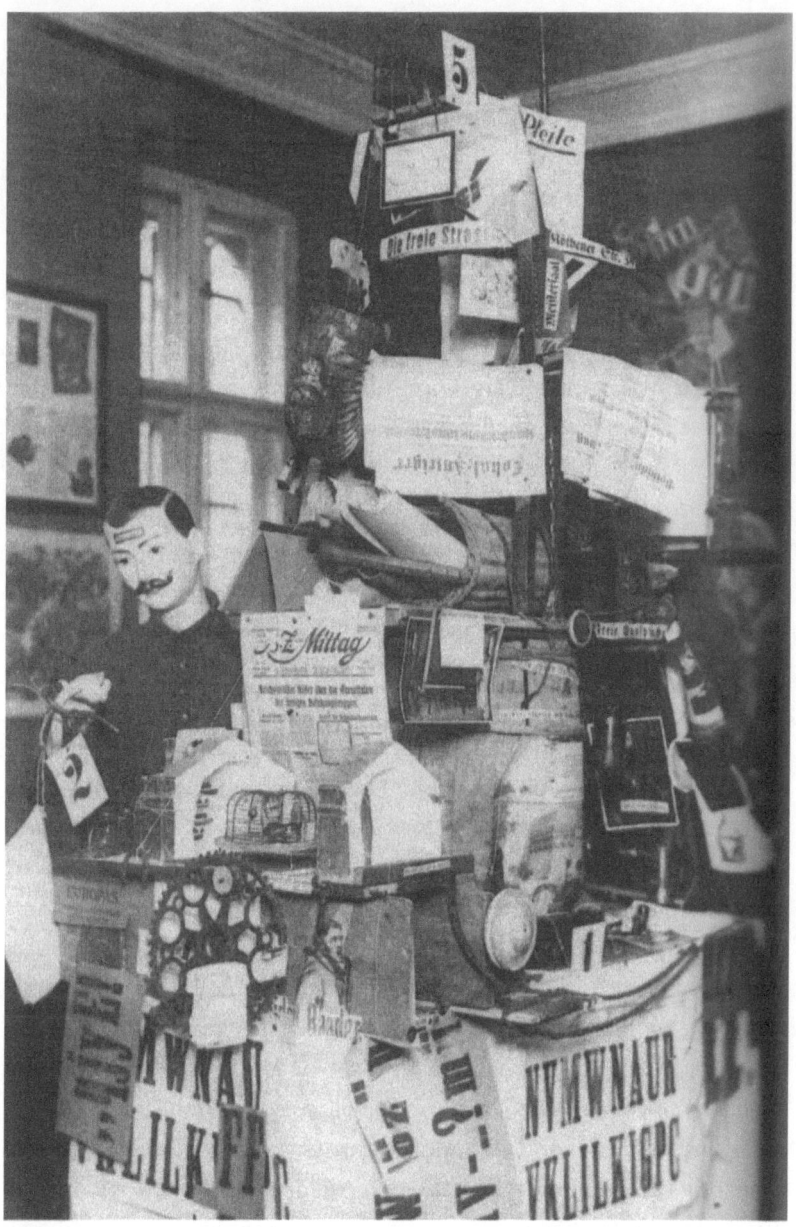

**FIGURE 15.** Photograph of Johannes Baader's assemblage *Great Plasto-Dio-Dada-Drama: Germany's Greatness and Decline*, First International Dada Fair, Berlin, 1920. Source: Catalog Dada, National Gallery of Art, Washington, 2006. Courtesy Andréi Nakov © Archive Nakov, Paris.

supposedly included "a museum of masterpieces through the ages," as well as copies of the Dada artist's own productions, old and recent. Higher still, Baader placed newspaper clippings about the war, which he declared to have been a purely journalistic invention. The top of the construction coincided with "the end of history," marked by the Last Judgment, which Baader announced that he himself had set off with the help of the worldwide revolution.[41] The perfect equivalence between the subject and his work—and between the artist's autobiography and the history of his country—is obvious in Figure 14, in which Baader stands just behind the mannequin. This *mise en abyme* of subjectivity clearly tested the boundaries between fiction and reality, facticity and truth. Not only was the mannequin Baader's double, but also Baader himself, in his constant switching of roles, turned out to be his own mannequin.

In fact, Baader, the megalomaniac artist, had appropriated a number of messianic identities of his time: he ran to represent Sarrebruck in the Reichstag, he founded the Freiheitspartei (Freedom Party), and in 1920 he wrote a tract titled "Dadaists Against Weimar," in which he proclaimed himself "President of the Terrestrial Globe." Having for years already identified himself with Christ, he announced his enthronement as well as his own death. These actions along with many others finally took their place in the logical field of ambivalence, of the indecision between seriousness and irony. Baader became the allegory of a country that had been promised glory but found itself reduced to ruins. He appropriated the jargon of Germany's self-appointed saviors, who proliferated during those years, as Max Weber pointed out with alarm in his 1917 speech "Science as Vocation." But at the same time, Baader also constructed the antimonument of this jargon.[42] Thus Sudhalter is right to insist on the critical dimension of Baader's *Plasto-Dio-Dada-Drama*, which she sees as an ironic retort to Germany's national monuments and, in particular, the *Völkerschlachtdenkmal* in Leipzig commemorating the German victory over Napoleonic France. But we may go further and allow ourselves to be carried (away) by the semiotic vertigo of Baader's actions. *Plasto-Dio-Dada-Drama* was an inverted monument to the traumatized memory that existed at three levels: the nation, Expressionism and its dream of cathedrals that could turn around the meaning of the defeat, and finally, Baader's own self.[43]

The assemblage's triple reference (to the nation, to the megalomaniac art of its time, and to Baader himself) raised the Futurist and Dadaist mechanism of converting pessimism into artificial optimism to the level of the absurd. Baader turned the commemorative monument, which was supposed to fix greatness in time, into a maniacal object of destruction and (self-)derision. Sudhalter, in her analysis of *Plasto-Dio-Dada-Drama*, insists on Baader's beginnings: he started his career as a specialist in funerary architecture (he belonged to the association of Dresden Plastic Artists for Sepulchral Paintings and worked for a funeral business until 1915). We should pursue this line of inquiry and examine the melancholy that infused the activities of an artist who dedicated his art to combating death and forgetting. We realize, then, that this artist, after designing a number of mausoleums and tombstones, fell increasingly victim to mania. He decided to incorporate the totality of history and lived experience into himself rather than allow himself to be devoured by them. Dada clearly constituted the paroxysmal moment of this mania.

At the beginning of the twentieth century, Baader's most steadfast mourning was undoubtedly for history, as his stylistic eclecticism and Wagnerian symbolism show. In an important text from 1906, dedicated to his utopian project for a "Monument to Humanity," Baader attributed to his edifice the qualities of all the significant monuments of human history, from Egyptian and Assyrian architecture to the more traditional architecture of Classical and Roman antiquity.[44] He was one of the many total artists living and working at the end of the nineteenth century who conceived colossal, utopian edifices that were supposed to encompass, and thus complete, all earthly civilizations, old and new, near and far. This historical current was one of utopian Expressionism's major references, and the artist Wenzel Hablik, one of the members of the Gläserne Kette (Crystal Chain), for example, never completely detached himself from it.[45]

The same totalizing tendency can be found in the duration of the monument's construction, which was supposed to stretch out over 1,000

years, and in its height, which was to reach 1,500 meters.[46] This architectural Wagnerism sought to exit the fluctuating time of modernity in
order to restore the *longue durée* (long duration), the temporal expression
of phantasmatic monumental totalities. But, of course, Baader's new totality fed off the disparate materials supplied by centuries of accumulated
history: he imagined the monument as a pyramid-shaped stratification
of styles from throughout history.[47] Unable to meet such requirements,
Baader's temple survives only as a sketch that vaguely associates pyramids
and Hindu temples.

Finally, one of the monument's many purposes (Baader's eclecticism
was not only stylistic but also functional) was to serve as a museum of
all the cultures of the world. Baader retained this obsessive eclecticism,
along with the devouring of history it implied, in his Dadaist assemblage,
but in a disenchanted way: he began pointing out the elective affinities
between history and the press. By summoning a reproducible past, he
transformed that noble segment of time into a mere fiction.

In short, no indexical proof was enough to secure the authenticity of
facts. Baader followed the endless spiral of performativity or madness,
both of which, after all, involve the same subjection of the object to
its emancipated sign. Who exactly was Johannes Baader, and what was
the history of Germany? Baader the Dadaist subjected his eclecticism to
the principle of *actualization*: if he could take on all the roles of the present, it was because by himself he was nothing. He wrote: "A Dadaist is
someone who lives life in all its forms, who knows it, and who says: not
only here, but also there, there, there is life."[48] This simultaneity operated not only synchronistically, absorbing the multiple qualities of modern man, but also diachronistically: "I have traversed every country and
every age in thought. There is neither past nor future for me"[49]—neither
the crushing past of our forefathers, nor any wandering through an unknown future, nor yet exhaustion in the fleeting present.

Guillaume Apollinaire advocated something similar in his defense of
Cubism, which was also one of the most ardent defenses of the religion
of art: "To do this we must encompass past, present, and future in a

single glance. The canvas must exhibit that essential unity which alone induces ecstasy."[50] Baader presented the frantic downward spiral of the artist's dream of becoming divine by mastering simultaneity. The frantic spiraling of divinization is also the key to his pseudonym, Oberdada (Superdada). With the "Ober" half of the name, Baader claimed, like God, to have accessed the eternal present, but with "dada" he admitted that he was an inconsistent and variable God. By slipping into reproducible time, Baader identified himself with the "furtively receding nothing"[51] of the present and became a mirror.[52]

Baader the Dadaist also left behind a project for a construction intended to last a thousand years. His works were to let themselves be absorbed by the flow of time, for they lacked any objective anchor in the real as it really happened. In his essay on photography, Kracauer considered the consequences of that medium on the status of works of art. Well before Walter Benjamin, Kracauer pointed out the contradiction that exists between the requirement that a work of art be original and its actual reproducibility.

> Artworks suffer this fate through their reproductions. The phrase "lie together, die together" applies to the multiply produced original; rather than coming into view through the reproductions, it tends to disappear in its multiplicity and to live on as art photography.[53]

Three years later, in 1930, the art historian Erwin Panofsky wrote his essay "Original and Facsimile Reproduction," in which he conceded an infinitely perfectible pedagogical value to reproductions, provided that the work of art never renounce its irreducible essence, "originality": "But should a time come when *no one* can make this distinction [between original and reproduction] anymore, when the work of man and the work of machine have effectively become *identical*, then it is not the *appreciation* of art, but *art* itself that has died."[54] The Dadaists shared Kracauer's and Panofsky's views equally. But unlike Kracauer, they did not deplore the death of a work of art through its photographic reproduction. And unlike Panofsky, they found infinite pleasure in proclaiming the death of a certain kind of art: human art built on the irreducible difference between the original and its copy, between monument and document.

In conclusion, the dams had burst and the floodwaters could carry away all they liked. There was the response of Baader: the double, triple, even quadruple play of ambivalence, protean subjectivity adapting to the flux of time. But Baader was one of a kind. Despite their differences, the other Berlin Dadaists did not give themselves over with abandon to the "furtively receding nothing" but tried to critically and constructively question the various segments of time: past, present, and future. It is this double nature of the Dadaists' work—critical and affirmative at once, combined with a good dose of historical materialism and an acute anthropological sensibility—that Roman Jakobson and others like him missed when they insisted only on the Dadaist devaluation of time and artworks, and it is this critical-affirmative dimension of modern reproducibility, with the utopian resources it contained, that escaped both the melancholic Kracauer and the humanist Panofsky.

# ART'S EFFICACY *OR* DADA'S USE VALUE

### Eternity: The Plus-Value of Time

Interpretations such as Jakobson's grasp Dada's gesture but ignore its function, they grasp its bluff but ignore the commitment inherent in it. These interpretations leave out the Dadaists' well-developed thoughts on the efficacy—whether good or bad, beneficial or harmful—that works of art can have. Even though they saw the classical or any other norm from the past as anachronistic, they considered its effects to still be *extremely present*. The semiotic ambivalence of Grosz and Heartfield's assemblage rests on an awareness of precisely this: on the one hand, *The Middle-Class Philistine Heartfield Gone Wild* signifies a sculpture from antiquity, admired in museums; on the other hand, it refers to an ordinary contemporary citizen taking shelter in his own private space as revolution rages in the streets of Berlin. The efficacy of classical sculpture lay in its ability to keep "the petit bourgeois John Heartfield" at home; conversely, the efficacy to which the Dadaist assemblage aspired consisted in causing the spectator to understand that ability.

One of the many objectives of Grosz and Heartfield's assemblage was to respond concretely and specifically—hence, through form—to the diatribes of Gertrud Alexander, art critic for the *Rote Fahne*, the official newspaper of the Communist Party.[1] They were responding, in particular, to the controversy that was sparked when an artillery shell hit the Dresden Gemälde Galerie during the fighting between workers and the Kapp putschists, destroying Rubens's *Baccanales* painting. The Dadaists defended the principle of political struggle and the unforeseeable damage it might cause over the *eternal* value of Great Art. They thereby disagreed with both the Expressionist Oskar Kokoscka, who dismissed the two political camps and defended the sacred autonomy of art, and the communist Alexander, who, despite her support for the working class, vigorously urged respect for the works of the past.

At bottom, the two Dadaists' argument was based on their idea, which they never explicitly stated, that temporal, social, and political *surpluses* and *plus-values* were inseparable from the cult of Great Art. We must look to the logic the communist critic Alexander used to support her argument to better understand the Dadaists' idea. Attempting to reconcile historical materialism with aesthetic idealism, Alexander conferred a double value on works of art: their *historical* value as documents (because every work of art testified to the economic and social conditions that determined its creation) and their *ahistorical* value as eternal. From its supposed creation by genius—an ahistorical quality by definition—a work of art's eternity value was more or less produced by its reception. Over the course of history, eternity value was passed down from one generation to the next and from one rising class to another. It was thus logical that the proletariat, the ultimate masters of history, would in turn want to appropriate this heritage. But, Alexander argued, to do so, they first had to learn to respect it.

It was this inheritability of artworks that the Dadaists violently contested, precisely because of the formidable efficacy they attributed to it. Grosz and Heartfield observed quite simply that the eternity in question, which I interpret here as a temporal plus-value, was the direct expression of the plus-value of the accumulated workers' labor: "Workers, you, who continually create the surplus value that allows the exploiters to hang their walls with this 'aesthetic luxury.'"[2] The process required for surplus value and aesthetic luxury was circular and involved two moments.

The first moment sees the work of art as a luxury; the surplus of illusion becomes something like the concretion of the surplus labor power expended by workers but confiscated by capital. The second moment sees the surplus of illusion finally turning against its source, that is, the workers. This vicious cycle, this nightmarish return of the same, guaranteed the anesthetizing efficacy of Great Art.[3] "What is art to the working man?" Grosz and Heartfield asked. "In the face of all these horrifying truths, art seeks to lead him into an ideal world where they do not apply; it strives to divert him from revolutionary action, to make him forget the crimes of the rich, and to hoodwink him into believing in the bourgeois notion of a world of order and tranquility."[4]

The biggest reproach that *The Middle-Class Philistine Heartfield Gone Wild* addressed to antiquity was that it cradled people in a world of order and tranquility far from the conflicts of their own time. Raoul Hausmann expressed the same idea in his criticism of "Weimarian classicism." This expression designated both the *Weimarklassik* and what Hausmann considered its avatars—Expressionism, for example—and the new German government, whose "sacred union" had been celebrated in the town of Weimar.

> The consequences of Goethe and Schiller were even more lamentable than those of old King Fritz, and the Ebert-Scheidemann government resulted from the foolishness and greed of Weimar classicism. This classicism is a uniform, a metric covering for things without a breath of life in them. Far from the whirlwind, of real events, serious poets, social-democrats, and democrats cover their irrelevance with the stiff drapery of their dignified decrees; interchangeable military monotonies give them airs of goodness and humanity.[5]

The metric costume for "things without a breath of life in them" was not just the aesthetic correlate or mere symptom of the coalition celebrated at the Weimar assembly. More significantly, this aesthetic uniform played an active role in creating German political reality. After all, the Weimar classicists transmitted their praise of interiority—something to be cultivated far from the turmoil of the public sphere—to Germany's *Bildungsbürgertum* (cultured middle class). Of course, a huge gulf lay between the original Weimar humanist cosmopolitanism and the nationalist pettiness that was brewing in the young republic. The separation between the two was total, but German nationalism incorporated the classics in its own way. The final chapter of the national bildungsroman was written on the front lines, where young soldiers brought the works of Goethe and Schiller with them to battle. This is why in 1920 the draperies of classicism, those counter-gaps that in their own way separated the real from the ideal, those concretions of energy charged with so much illusion, could be deployed both in art (as in Expressionism) and in politics (the Weimar assembly). And the Dadaist montage was the instrument that made these classical trappings visible—by tearing them to shreds.

## The Rhetoric of Antiphrasis
## and the Function of the Montage

The beautiful appearances of Grosz and Heartfield's assemblage were indeed slashed and torn, laying bare the delicate human body that had been torn to pieces by its recent adventures (see Figure 10). The Dadaist assemblage had been "shaken"; this was the expression Walter Benjamin used to describe the destruction of the "authenticity" and "originality" of the work of art.[6] In this particular case, the assemblage's replaceable and fragmented form and its display among a crowd of more or less ephemeral objects provided ample evidence.[7] Somewhat ironically, the old, long-standing ambition of the idealist aesthetic—to achieve total transparency of content in form—was realized literally in this work, where miserable form perfectly expressed moral disposition.

Less transparent, however, was the staging of the work and its reception. The two artists and their friend Schmalhausen had themselves photographed in deep contemplation of their work (see Figure 8). I interpret this pose as an antiphrasis that, by contrasting the aggressive form of the assemblage with its candid and affable reception, prolonged the semiotic ambivalence of the work itself. As the work's creators, Grosz and

Heartfield renounced all traces of aura, but as spectators, they pretended to be completely absorbed in imperturbable meditation. A work made of reproducibility itself is shown to afford a unique experience; a work made of the agonies of its time is presented as capable of suspending time. And time literally stopped, with the simple click of a camera. The photographic click became the ironic reversal of eternity.

The work's semiotic ambivalence, which extended to this staging of its contemplative reception, forcefully affirmed the Dadaists' desire to give the work of art a function altogether opposite from the autonomy usually celebrated in private or museum viewing spaces. This point allows us to understand the semantic charge of the other half of the photograph, where Hausmann, Baader, and Burchard cultivate distraction (see Figure 8). They are shown conversing, with their backs to their artworks. They demonstrate that they hold no excessive respect for their creations, and they display their conviction that the transformation of subjectivity is a complex affair, requiring all modes of expression: works and words, speculation and action. Above all, the three men show that for them, the major ontological goal of their work is to forge relations. Whereas on the right side of the photograph, the cultic work of art absorbs all individual energy, turning the spectator into something as rigid, closed, and independent as the piece itself (and this inverted mimesis is indeed the horizon of its efficacy), on the left side, the work of art and its distracted presentation suggest open, social, modifiable attitudes.

This meant that art had to renounce its former idealizing and thus narcissistic function and turn to what Hausmann called the "practical detoxification" of the subject.[8] As early as 1918, when Hausmann realized that Dada could offer the materialist grounding necessary for his own still fairly idealist search for a subjectivity woven of *Ich* and *Wir*, he wrote of his "sincere desire to show his own situation without embellishment"[9] and defended "tearing down the notion of art in favor of perception and simultaneous experience."[10] Already in 1912, André Salmon had written regarding Cubism that "the smile of the Mona Lisa was, for too long perhaps, art's shining sun."[11] Whereas Picasso took inspiration from

African sculpture for his work against art's idealizing postulate, the Berlin Dadaists turned to what they called the new material, that is, any kind of fragment—objects, printed or phonetic matter—they could extract directly from reality. To be sure, this new material dated back to Cubism. But in Cubist collages it lost all its value as object or as real and was integrated into a cognitive game of continuous reflection on the fuzzy limits between reality and representation, form and content, object and sign, positive and negative. Dadaist montages, on the other hand, performed a task more anthropological and political than logical: by returning to the object, they intended to represent the always-open (for better or worse) relations between man and his milieu, mind and matter, art and life.

Dadaists shared this aspiration to put an end to anthropomorphism with Carl Einstein, and it formed the basis of their political mutual understanding. When representation of the world would finally cease to be an indirect representation of man, man would perhaps learn to live "auf eigene Kosten" (at his own expense), as Hausmann and his friend Franz Jung wrote. The bourgeoisie (both as a class and as a moral disposition), its political system (parliamentary democracy), and its favorite mode of artistic expression (imitation) had always functioned through and at the expense of the Other, whether man or object.[12] *Auf eigene Kosten* was the meaning of the self-possession to which the Dadaists aspired. It was also a key dimension of Dadaist primitivism, which we should now begin to seriously take into account. It also, finally, defined their sense of the present.

In his highly illuminating manuscript on Dadaist primitivism titled "Schöpfung und Entwicklung" (Creation and Evolution), Ludwig Hilberseimer wrote:

> One suddenly understood the fundamental importance of primitiveness as against that reproductiveness that turned into habituation and dominion over materials, killed will-power, and saw good in the mere development of knowledge and the work of art.[13]

In its fight against the reproductiveness of art, Dadaist primitivism found a natural intercessor in pure reproducibility. Thus Dada declared that the imitative or historicist quality of reproducibility could be overcome. Walter Benjamin would see in Dadaism's barbarisms the will to include the consequences of mechanical reproducibility in the work of art itself.[14] The Dada Messe in the summer of 1920 was a heightened manifestation of these barbarisms. In its fierce defense of art's use value, the exposition—which was violently attacked for having destroyed the privileged status of works of art—reactivated art's magical function, adapting it to the demands of the present.

# THE MOMENT OF DECISION

## The Future-from-Now

### The Death of Art: Decentering Achieved

Another famous photograph has come down to us from the Dada Messe (Figure 16). Like the photograph showing the Berlin Dadaists divided between contemplation and distraction (Figure 8), it is no simple document. Here, only two Dadaists are shown: the Marxists George Grosz and John Heartfield, who pose for the camera holding a placard that reads "Die Kunst ist tot. Es lebe die neue Maschinenkunst TATLINS" ("Art is dead. TATLIN'S new machine art lives.")

This second photograph is the opposite and dialectical complement of the first in every respect. Here, both artists' backs are to their assemblage, but they are not looking at the camera. Instead, they observe each other with complicity, as though in the middle of coming to an agreement. Their appearance is impeccable: Grosz has the sleeves of his white shirt rolled up and is wearing a hat and tie; Heartfield is in his black suit. Both men are smoking.

Whereas the first photograph showed the artists lost in contemplation of their work, here, Grosz and Heartfield take on the role of active artists, completely confident in the choice they have made. This is why they have their backs to their assemblage: they are going forward, and their stance

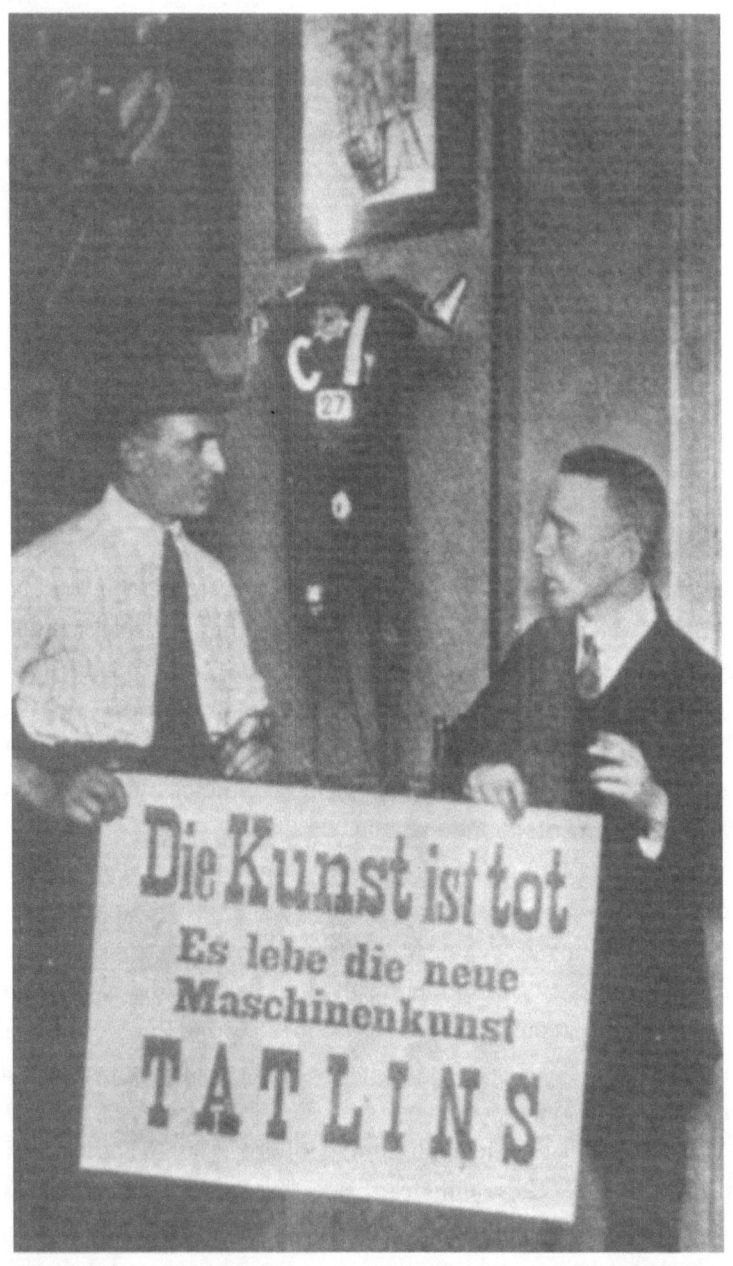

**FIGURE 16.** George Grosz (left) and John Heartfield. Source: Photograph originally published in Richard Huelsenbeck, *Dada Almanach*, Berlin, 1920.

signals that their practices will henceforth be directed toward goals other than the critical deconstruction of autonomous art. They are looking at each other as though to give the start signal. If their contemplative posture before their assemblage in the first photograph was an antiphrasis, their determined attitude in the second photograph is a direct affirmation. Dadaist ambivalence and hide-and-seek will be replaced by communist univocity, based on the postulate of the transparency of history. If this hypothesis is correct, it also means that with this photograph, Grosz and Heartfield announced the end of their involvement with Dada. This end was a *decision*, an *Entscheidung*, a concept that would go on to have a major, complex role in the shocks that democracy received during the Weimar Republic.[1]

The Dadaists' decision was first manifested in their definitive renunciation of the autonomy of art, including the moment of its deconstruction, in favor of art's service to the communist utopia. Today, it is well-known that Grosz and Heartfield's announcement of the end of art was inspired by the Russian critic Konstantin Umanskij, who, in a series of 1920 articles in the journal *Ararat* (later collected and published as a small book), presented Tatlinism as the integration of technology into works of art.

> Art is dead. Long live art, machine art, with its construction and its logic, its rhythm, its elements, its material, its metaphysical spirit—the art of counter-relief. The latter finds no material unworthy. Wood, glass, paper, sheet metal, iron, screws, nails, electrical fixtures, shards of glass . . . all this will be presented as legitimate means of artistic expression, and art's new grammar and aesthetic require the artist to forge stronger connections with its powerful ally, the magnificent machine. A triumph of intellect and matter, the negation of the mind's right to autonomy, the quintessence of contemporary reality—victorious materialism—this is how we must explain the art of counter-reliefs, which for the first time has put between quotation marks such "sacred words" as "art," "painting," "picture."[2]

It is clear that the Dadaists inverted Umanskij's logic here, for instead of seeing Tatlinism as the integration of technology into art, they saw it as the dissolution of art into technology, broadly understood.

They did so because, like many other artists of their time—for example, the constructivists and Mondrian—the Dadaists interpreted the death of art as a process of ontological decentering that could potentially eradicate the false division inherent in metaphysics and thus lead to the synthesis of intellect and material. Here is how Hausmann explained the trajectory of modern art in 1921:

> The old art was a construction, a synopsis arranged in absolutist fashion around a center. The new art is a decentralization, a decomposition of the center, a dissolution. This leads either to the end of all art or to an entirely new art in which notions common today, the nostalgia for seeing the world through the lens of human will—as if it were a product of man's imagination—and identifying it with reality, no longer have any value.[3]

For the Dadaists the decentering of art and the subject would take two forms: first, social struggle, which, in keeping with the Saint-Simonian model of art, considered art a means of propaganda or consciousness raising; and second, more romantic in content and abstract, the inauguration of a "horizontality of relations," meaning a harmony between form and technology, at the level of cities, communities, and, even and above all, the universe itself. The task of the artist would be to weave these relations with and for others. Hausmann's decision was to pursue the objectivization of horizontality rather than to serve the revolution, for he believed that violence could be spared so long as one could detect the liberating possibilities discreetly lodged in the present. This is why he named his own decisional vision presentism. His vision, which combined horizontality and the present, was considerably more compatible with Weimar Republic capitalism and social democracy than was the communist vision of Grosz and Heartfield.

## Art as Propaganda:
## "Reactionary and Revolutionary in One,
## a Symbol of the Times"

On February 5, 1919, Count Harry Kessler visited George Grosz's studio and saw his painting *Germany, A Winter's Tale* (now lost) (see Figure 9). The regime of simultaneity that governs this composition strips objects of their corporeal integrity, with the notable exception of the bourgeois man at the center of the painting, who, supported by the three allegorical figures of church, army, and education, maintains his compactness. Seated at his table, he is caught in the endless cycle of his own self-preservation; with the remains of his meal still on his plate and already holding his cutlery in antic-ipation, he casts his hunter's gaze on the world moving around him. Grosz probably did not discuss this relationship between a fragmented though liv-ing object and a compact but almost fossilized subject with Count Kessler. He preferred, instead, to emphasize the moralistic aspect of his painting, even revealing his ambition to become the "German Hogarth." He created his painting, he said, as though it would be hung in schools.

When Count Kessler remarked on the intrinsically wasteful nature of art, which made it so unsuitable for any utilitarian purpose, Grosz retorted that "art as such is unnatural, a disease, and the artist a man possessed. Mankind can do without art."[4] According to Kessler, Grosz's arguments stemmed from a pictorial Bolshevism that was paradoxical in its attempt to revive the art of the distant past (Hogarth, religious painting). Thus, by combining utopia and restoration, Grosz was "reactionary and revolution-ary in one, a symbol of the times."[5] Whereas the artist's revolutionary side was confirmed by his war against the autonomy of art, his reactionary side was revealed in his goal of restoring art's supposed former educational function, as, for example, when it had been used to explain the Bible on church walls.[6]

Years later, Wieland Herzfelde recalled that he and his brother, John Heartfield, owed their "detoxification" from the Expressionism of their youth to George Grosz, a blasé artist if ever there was one. We might suppose that Grosz himself found the means for his own practical detoxification from a maniac or possessed man in Dadaism's mimetic practices. Once the apotropaic process had been completed, he was ready—purged and henceforth imperturbable—to dedicate himself to the rational mission of communism.

Does this mean that in the end, Dada was no more than a simple therapeutic formula or strategy for combat? Of course not. There is a strict complementarity between the two antithetical postures of critical contemplation and affirmative action, between the defense of the present and the utopia of the future. If we examine the first photograph in isolation (Figure 8), we must acknowledge that its critical presentism may contradict communist utopia; its goal is to defend the sovereignty of the present against past *and* future alike. But if we examine the same picture in relation to the second one (Figure 16), in which Grosz and Heartfield proclaim the end of art, all logical contradiction disappears, neutralized by the start signal the two artists give each other. Their exchange of looks contains their decision.[7] And this decision leaps from the present to the future, virtually projecting the bodies of the two artists into action. The decision—antithetical to both the wait-and-see attitude typical of socialism and to any nostalgia for a lost object— seizes the present, which, in its ecstatic opening, dilates into the future. Thus the decision is compatible with photography: it strives to be just as *immediate* as the photographic click. This means that the Dadaists explored the specificity of photography not only in an attempt to deconstruct traditional history but also to give form to their active conception of history. Action was not something to come, as the social-democratic utopias sabotaging the will of history would have it; it had already been set off, like the click of a camera.

In 1922, two years after the Dada Messe, the publishing house Malik Editions—headed, as we know, by Wieland Herzfelde—published György Lukács's *History and Class Consciousness*. The book was a defense of the present ("We consider the problem of the present," Lukács wrote, "as a historical problem"[8]) against the abstract future so characteristic of utopia. It was also a response to Ernst Bloch's *Spirit of Utopia* (1918), in which Bloch attempted to transform the opaque present into the holder of utopia. It is clear that the future's backward leap into the present greatly interested Lukács, who, in his determination to dissipate all mystical ambiguity surrounding how the revolution would arrive, insisted on the role of mediation. For Lukács, the false immediacy of the present could be cleared away by fighting against the inertia of the past and the disorientation created by an abstract future; awareness of the mediations composing the present should coincide with a decision.

> When the concrete here and now dissolves into a process it is no longer a continuous, intangible moment, immediacy slipping away; it is the focus of the deepest and most widely ramified mediation, the focus of *decision* and of the birth of the new. As long as man concentrates his interest contemplatively upon the past or future, both ossify into an alien existence. And between the subject and the object lies the unbridgeable "pernicious chasm" of the present. Man must be able to comprehend the present as a becoming. He can do this by seeing in it the tendencies out of whose dialectical opposition he can *make* the future. Only when he does this will the present be a process of becoming, that belongs to *him*. Only he who is willing and whose mission it is to create the future can see the present in its concrete truth.[9]

This is almost exactly the Marxist Dadaists' approach to art: because concentrating on either the past or the future resulted in the fossilization of life, the present had to be transformed from a pernicious chasm into what we might call a mediated gap. For them, mediation was a matter of montage, either visible or camouflaged.

**Utopian Presentism:**
**The Horizontality of Relations**

Hausmann's pact with communism during the Spartacist revolution was true but temporary; he found it a necessary response to the violence of history. In his contempt for the transcendent and autonomous subject, the anarchist Hausmann thought he could not stand on the sidelines of revolutionary turmoil as supposedly democratic parties concluded their own pacts with the far right.[10] However, he never went so far as to adopt communism's historical teleology. He clung instead to his own vision of history as obeying only the principles of identity and contradiction. Along with several other artists associated with Dada—Kurt Schwitters and Tristan Tzara, for example—he declared himself infinitely skeptical about proletarian art, whose subject, object, and audience he found difficult to define.[11] No doubt he also found that communist teleology devalued the present, just as it remained fundamentally humanist and thereby elided the decentered experience of Dadaism.

All signs indicate that Hausmann was not convinced of the soundness of Grosz and Heartfield's decision. This, however, was not his attitude toward Huelsenbeck, of whom he wrote, "The only modern man in this country, Richard Huelsenbeck, has withdrawn into obscurity—let us respect his silence!"[12] What Hausmann did not say was that the flip side of Huelsenbeck's silence on the present was his authoritative word on the past: in keeping with the classic image of the historian, the ex-Dadaist withdrew into the obscurity of the past in order to write *the histories* of Dada.

As for Hausmann, he found in his new theory, which he simply called presentism, the solution that allowed him to exit Dada without denying it. That was in 1921. He tempered the polemical aspect of the present to which he turned and attempted to emphasize its emancipatory potential.

> In the monstrous dusk surrounding us, which weighs on our hearts and minds because it may turn either to light or dark—in this instant, let us make an energetic decision! We want light, light that penetrates all bodies, we do not want to let the delicate and relationship-rich emanations go to ruin before our tired eyes; we want, with light, the great undiscovered America, LIFE!![13]

Once again, the present had to be torn from its crepuscular position between memory and waiting, light and dark. In exact antithesis to Orlando, who felt saved by crepuscular *indecision* from the brutality of the suddenly revealed present, Hausmann wanted to slice through intermediary time by exercising choice: "Let us make an energetic decision," he exclaimed. This Hausmannian sunset was the individual, biographical equivalent of the zone of interpenetration between post- and prehistory at the macroscopic level of history. Undoubtedly, Hausmann had decided it was time to stop surviving and start living. Whereas the mimetic practices of Dadaism had been techniques for surviving the adversities of a second prehistory, Hausmann's presentism was meant to give full access to the experience of life. True, achieving this required, first, transfiguring the present through a good dose of mysticism and a specific political vision. In any event, the Dadaist sunset split into night and day: Huelsenbeck chose the night of history, and Hausmann opted for the light of the present.

In both cases the observation was the same and had been expressed by Saint Augustine, who, confronted with the aporia of the present, wrote in his *Confessions* that the present is time "that only exists because it is on its way to non-existence."[14] As for Hausmann, he realized that retrospective and prospective utopias alike contributed to hollowing out the present. That was their great paradox; by pulling a subject toward the past or the future, they turned the present into the only America on which humans had never set foot. Dada's critical presentism fought hard against the accumulation of the past and the abstraction of the future, but Hausmann's utopian presentism wanted only to explore the plenitude of the present. This, no doubt, was hugely ambitious. It was the eschatological dream of "a full and immediate presence closing history, the transparence and indivision of a parousia," to quote Jacques Derrida.[15] Hausmann's project for phonetic poetry fit (though more ambiguously than Hugo Ball's) within the Christian tradition of the pneumatic word, pure breath, which Derrida contrasted to his own grammatological thought.[16]

Bettina Schaschke has focused on Hausmann's pneumatology by connecting his thoughts on phonetic poetry to the tires (*pneus*) in his photomontage *Elasticum* (1920).[17] Here is Hausmann in his "Manifesto on the Law of Sound": "The tires of the transcendental-immanent car-soul are inflated with the force of a compressed resistance capacity akin to that of Benzol."[18] Whereas Ball used phonetic poetry as a means of initiation into pure pneuma—a Gnostic notion he analyzed in his theological stud-ies during the 1920s—Hausmann, rather like Kurt Schwitters, chose to walk the razor's edge.[19] Without denying mechanical reproducibility, as the Expressionists had, he sought to transform it into a unifying force; without forgetting the banality of his time, he sought to uncover its uto-pian potential. His conception of the new man was also part of this logic.

The subject of presentism was, quite logically, a new man, ahistori-cal and thus free of fear: "The new man must have the courage to be new," wrote Hausmann.[20] Here again, Hausmann remained faithful to Christian eschatology; pneumatic poetry could only be offered up by a new man, one who had left behind divided language, marked by the writing of history, and it could only be the auditory expression of light, having reduced crepuscular uncertainty to nothing. This was the second step of Dadaist heroism: the transformation of the struggle for *survival* into a struggle for *life*. No doubt, the new man was poor in experience, in the sense in which Benjamin would later use the term, but he was also a primitive or first man.

Several historical signs convinced Hausmann of the topicality of this primitive figure, above all, the emergence of the proletariat as a historical actor. Between 1913 and 1920 Carl Einstein frequently expressed this very idea. He saw the proletariat's poverty as ultimately salvational, inasmuch as their lack of material possessions meant that they also lacked hab-its attached to such possessions. For Hausmann as well, the proletariat had lived *auf eigene Kosten*; because they had not been able to live by means of and at the expense of others (whether other humans or objects), they could easily achieve self-possession, which was also the possession of the present.[21] This is why Hausmann described the new man as a block of energy: contact with objects had not yet shaped or polished him. A rough stone, the first man was quite simply capable of anything; all possible actions lay before him. This logic—which of course was in-sufficiently materialist in postulating a primitive rather than alienated, poverty—separated Raoul Hausmann and Carl Einstein from Lukács's historical materialism.

## Despotic Milieu/Dreamed-of Milieu

How was Hausmann's presentism expressed in his works, and what, according to the artist, were the precise modalities of its advent? To answer this, I focus on a pencil sketch from 1920 made in connection with Hausmann's 1920 assemblage *Mechanical Head* (Figures 17 and 18). In the right foreground of the drawing (Figure 18), we see the oval head of an automaton, one of the many populating the Dadaist universe. If we look closely, however, we see that this head is that of the mannequin used in George Grosz's ambiguous celebration of his own marriage, the watercolor *Daum Marries Her Pedantic Automaton George in May 1920*, which was exhibited at the Dada Messe and which Herzfelde briefly commented on in the accompanying catalogue (Figure 19).

The differences between Grosz's and Hausmann's works are significant and highly instructive. Unlike Grosz's mannequin, which is cut off at the level of the genitals by the edge of the composition, Hausmann's stops just where the chest would start. Grosz's intention was to criticize social pressure exerted, in particular through the institution of marriage, on the sexual urges of the (male) subject, whereas Hausmann's goal was to explore the cerebral relations between the subject and its milieu. However, the same discrepancy between the top and the bottom halves of the head characterizes both works: the top half is white, only barely shaded at the contours, whereas the lower half is penciled in. The eyes of both mannequins are similarly empty, a bit like those ancient statues that Hegel, in his *Lectures on Aesthetics*, said lacked all inner being.[22] A measuring stick divides both foreheads and runs where a nose would be. Atop the head of Grosz's automaton, a pair of crossed female hands sits like the dove of the Holy Spirit, suggesting the role of women in men's alienation. There is nothing of the sort in Hausmann's drawing, which has no allegorical intention. In an interior depicted from a warped perspective, the little automaton George Grosz sits still, next to a woman significantly larger than him. The naturalness of the woman—implied by her undulating curves, the twisting of her body, and her visible genitalia—is in striking contrast to the automaton's impassiveness.

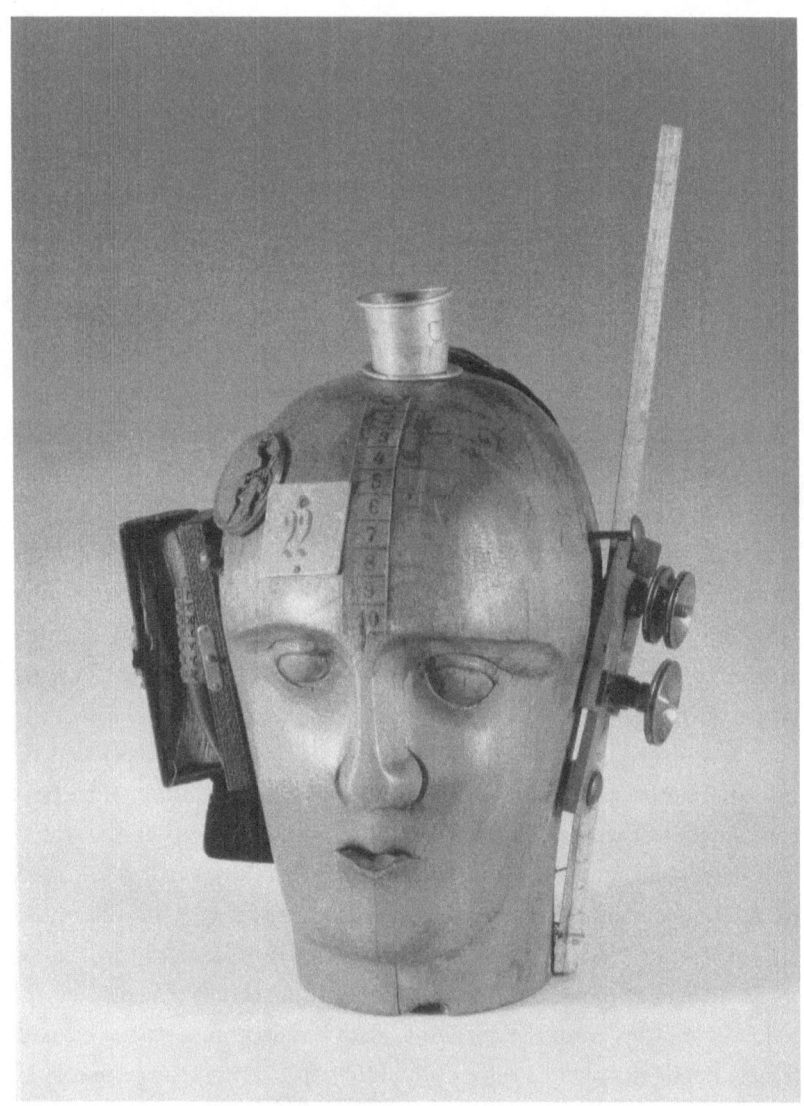

**FIGURE 17.** Raoul Hausmann, *Mechanischer Kopf* (*Der Geist unserer Zeit*) (Mechanical Head [The Spirit of our Age]), c. 1920, hairdresser's wig-making dummy, crocodile wallet, ruler, pocket-watch mechanism and case, bronze segment of old camera, typewriter cylinder, segment of measuring tape, collapsible cup, the number 22, nails, and bolt, 32.5 × 21 × 20 cm; Centre Pompidou, MNAM, Paris. Source: Catalog Dada, National Gallery of Art, Washington, 2006. © ADAGP, Paris 2015.

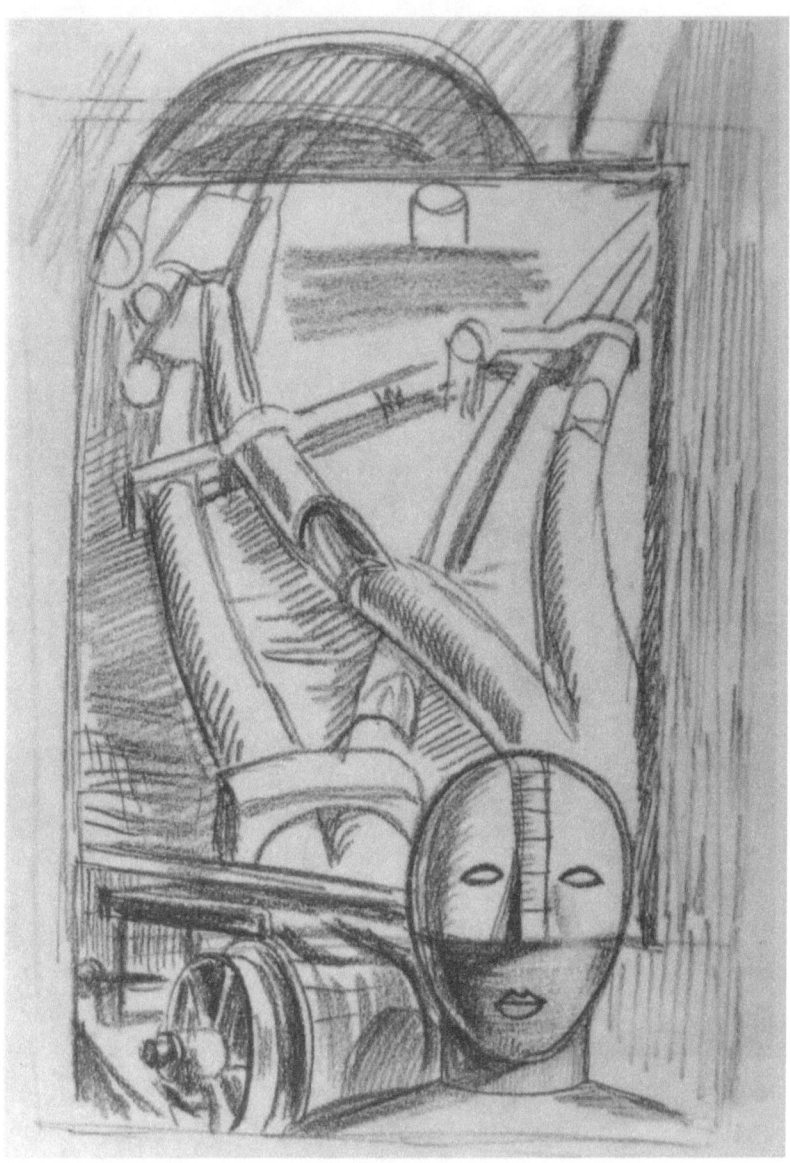

**FIGURE 18.** Raoul Hausmann, study for "Mechanical Head (Der Geist unserer Zeit)," c. 1920, chalk on paper, 25.7 × 17 cm; Berlinische Galerie, Berlin. Source: Catalog Dada, National Gallery of Art, Washington, 2006. © ADAGP, Paris 2015.

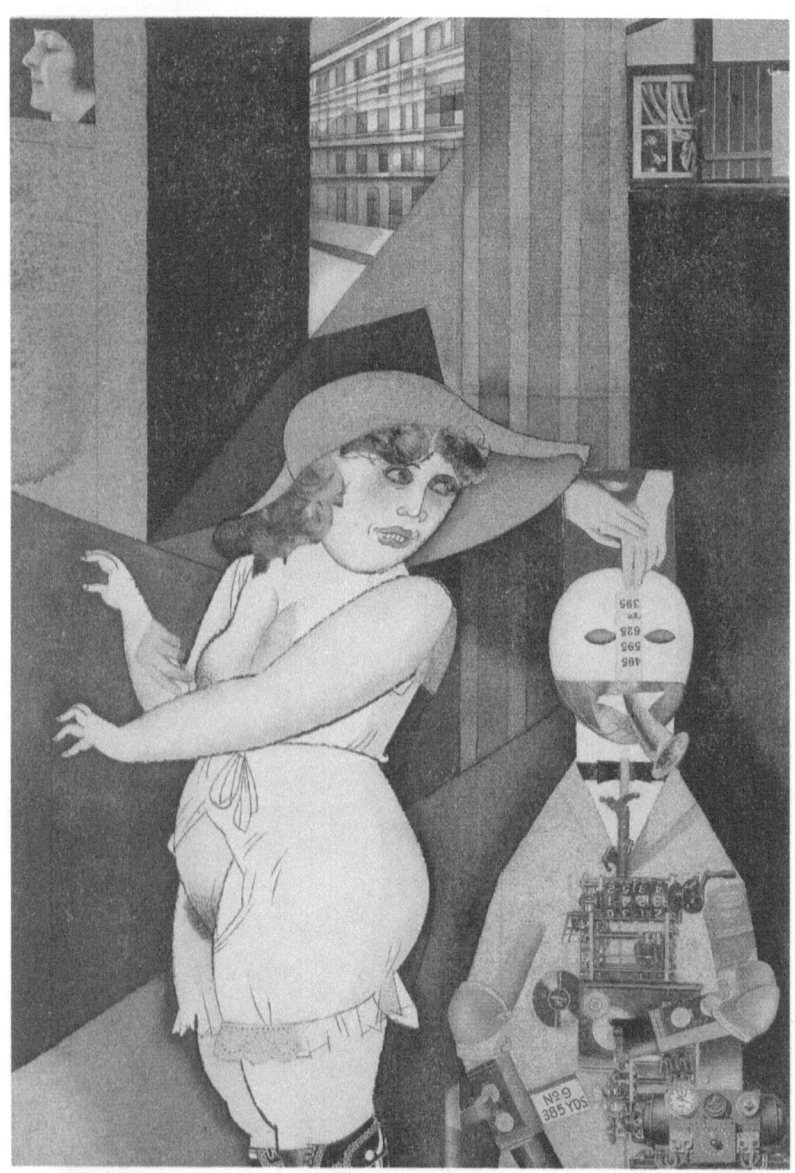

**FIGURE 19.** George Grosz, *"Daum" marries her pedantic automaton "George" in May 1920, John Heartfield is very glad of it (Meta-Mech. Constr. Nach Prof. R. Hausmann)*, 1920, watercolor, pencil, and ink on paper with photomontage and collage, 42 × 30.2 cm (16 ⁹⁄₁₆ × 11 ⁷⁄₈ inches); Berlinische Galerie, Berlin. Source: catalog Dada, National Gallery of Art, Washington, 2006. © The Estate of George Grosz, Princeton, N.J. / ADAGP, Paris 2015.

For Grosz, as for many avant-garde artists of the time, there was a perfect split in the world between matter and mind, between nature and technology, between woman and man. Grosz's watercolor delivers a value judgment on the role of women in producing social conventions, but there is no such judgment in Hausmann's drawing, which aspires to neutrality and indifference.

The drawing explores the indifference or indetermination that, according to Hausmann, emanated from the social, economic, and intellectual conditions of the age. He replaces Grosz's warped perspective with the neutral and impassive horizontality of a network—which by definition is used to create circulation. One of the branches of this network, forming behind the head, can easily be read as an extension of the nervous system of the head itself (see Figure 18). The equivalence between the subject's brain and the network of its milieu is also suggested by their plastic homology: the top part of the head and the network extending behind and within it receive the same linear treatment, barely shaded at the edges. Finally, the composition completes the drawing's perceptive complexity: a single line runs horizontally across the head and frames the entire network.

These three vectors of plastic ambivalence confirm that the head is an integral part of the network. But what is the nature of its integration? What relations does it imply between the subject and its milieu? Is the brain subject to the milieu, determined by it as despotically as Orlando was by her surroundings when she suddenly found herself in that London department store? Or, inversely, is the milieu something that emanates from the brain, like a dream? Is the subject with the absent gaze the author and agent of a virtual world? This undecidable ambivalence is the heart of Hausmann's presentism. It is precisely because man is permeable to his milieu that he is subject to its despotic power, but this also means that he can exercise his own action on it. The mechanical head in the 1920 drawing is not looking at the rational, abstract world; it does not face this world but rather belongs to it. The head dreams or thinks the world as much as it is thought by it.

In other words, on the one hand, there is the pole of necessity, the materialist determination of the human spirit: "What's the point of a mind in a world that just goes on mechanically?" asked Hausmann the Dadaist. "You see, you imagine that you think and make decisions. You imagine you are original—and what happens? Your surroundings, this rather dusty atmosphere, have set the soul's motor in motion and it all runs of itself. . . . You are simply being played on."[23] The supposed origin of the world, the artist-genius—quintessence of the autonomous subject—turns out to be merely an effect of it. But, on the other hand, there is the pole of freedom: the possibility for the subject to distance him- or herself from devouring matter and to use his or her own power against it. As Hausmann wrote in his manifesto on presentism:

> Man has two essential tendencies: one toward the impossible and the other toward all the innumerable possibilities. . . . We want to limit ourselves to the ineffable and nurturing possible! We want to connect the moment to its multiple emanations and to be transformed into living beings by the entire *possible*, which through mechanical consciousness, bold inventions, the realization of ideas, and the spirit (because nothing else deserves to be called "Spirit") transforms life into an engineer armed with its multiple capacities.[24]

Hausmann replaced the ideal—by definition, asymptotic—with the subject's capacity to detect the multiple emanations of the present. The present was a horizontal temporality, similar to the network whose multiple emanations stretch out behind the mechanical head. Hausmann replaced the verticality of the past and future fleeing into the infinite with a present expressed in multiple relations. Hausmann's decision was to convert bad into good; if, as Koselleck would later write, the present remains slippery, impossible to experience because of the ever-new unknowns that render it increasingly complex, Hausmann concluded that it was therefore necessary for oneself to become as fluid, as complex, and as differentiated as the present itself.

This amounts to saying that Hausmann's solution was the same as that of the constructivist abstract avant-gardes of the 1920s. Hence it would not be an exaggeration to say, inversely, that the avant-gardes who sought to create a perception on par with technology were *presentist*. The goal was to achieve sensorial amplification capable of grasping the complexity of the present. The lessons of second prehistory continued, though less terrifying than before; a certain reading of the present—in particular, of the relations or emanations comprising it—had intervened. These relations (*Beziehungen*) not only were an objective to be reached but also served as a sort of veil that allowed the avant-gardes of the 1920s to reconcile themselves to reality. These avant-gardes were ready to see in modern rationalization, division of labor, and, more generally, the economic and social relations of their time an interdependent reality that could discreetly correct the excesses of capitalism from within. The division of labor and time were transfigured into visions of collectivity and solidarity, which had won out over the egoism of autonomous work.

In 1920 and 1921 Hausmann began planning grandiose sound and light projects. His "optophonetic" theory was sustained by a mixture of scientism and mysticism, but it was also based on his political understanding of relations.

> We want to decenter our restrictive and object-riveted gaze, because our gaze, enlarged by science, has become round and full, because we have historically absorbed all optical possibilities and we are pursuing optics down to the essential phenomena of light. We love light and its movement![25]

Hausmann hoped that future technological progress would allow man to experience a universe in which "there will no longer be anything but relations of tension, relations between elements of color or elements of form."[26] For some years already, the artist had been following the ideas of the physician Ernst Moses Marcus, whose theory of ex-centric perception posited a decentered vision diffused over the entire surface of the skin. What better objection to the much-reviled *ocular* view could Hausmann have hoped for? Whereas man had previously stood *facing* the object, inventing perspective and other *ocular* tricks in a vain attempt to reduce the distance between himself and the object, *tactile* vision implied the abolition of this distance and possession of a disobjected world.[27]

Thus, to conclude, Hausmann wanted to replace the metaphysical and political model of hierarchical verticality with a horizontal model of solidarity.[28] From a temporal point of view, this meant uncoupling the fatal, necessary relationship between freedom and the future. From an ontological point of view, it meant the end of anthropocentric instrumentalization of the world. From the point of view of the status of the artist, it meant that Kandinsky's mystical triangle, with the artist at the top and the masses spread out along the base, disappeared. For Hausmann, a true descendant of Baudelaire, for whom the modern hero was clothed in black garb, signaling equality,[29] "even the most valorous man or the highest thought never surpasses what is known to all." And he added, "No one can ever conceive ideas that have not already been conceived and exist in society."[30] And because the most brilliant ideas and possibilities for historical change already existed, hidden in ordinary reality, not transcendent to it, the appropriate mode of perception for this reality was no longer pyramidal vision but rather ex-centric tactility.

It goes without saying that Hausmann's presentism, with its mystical scientism and its compromise with the magnified real, departed once and for all from the materialism of Grosz and Heartfield, who were hostile to idealizing the division of labor as anything other than relations of production—at least, they were hostile to this idealization as it was commonly practiced in capitalist society. And yet, if the two Marxist artists were drawn by communist utopia toward the future, Hausmann's mystical scientism, which was strongly allied with technological progress, did not futurize less his presentism. Despite everything, optophonetics existed in the separate, floating land of utopia. On the one hand, Hausmann praised the conventional, the uninteresting, the ordinary.[31] He considered that the artist's sole task was to connect the "multiple manifestations of the age, to formulate the new conventionality of clear and simple life."[32] The conventional artist could intervene as a publicist, stylist, or essayist. Thus, much like Adolf Loos in "Crime and Ornament," as well as many other authors writing in the same vein, Hausmann denounced artists' attempts to spiritualize the cinema and the Werkbund's bids to make life more interesting.[33] But, on the other hand, Hausmann distanced himself from the ordinary by turning to technology to accelerate, here and now, his ex-centric and interconnected cosmic vision.

# THE PARADIGM OF
# IMMACULATE CONCEPTION
## Between Fiction and History

**IT IS UNDENIABLE** that Dada was acutely aware of the history of its time. It was equally aware of its own place in history—the history of its time as well as history more generally. This was one of the major tensions running through Dada: no other movement had so insistently declared its noncapitalizable historical nature, and no other movement counted so many historiographers among its numbers.[1] The Dadaists wrote their history quickly and frenetically. Moreover, in keeping with their double posture in relation to history, they claimed with equal force the ephemeral, resolutely unrecoverable nature of their movement and eternity. Thus Hausmann and Huelsenbeck affirmed the historical unity of Dadaist practice while at the same time exalting its perfect adaptability to time. For them, Dada was both unique and reproducible. Ultimately, Dada is as ephemeral and eternal as the present, which never dies even though everything it contains is mortal. In its quest to seize the present, Dada hoped to die and be reborn as much as, and with, the present. Such was the movement's self-reflexive presentism, which undoubtedly explains Hausmann's strange mixture of materialism and mysticism. A harsh critic of his own historical present, he was no less inclined to see this same present as a slice of eternity. Similarly, we can see the two poles of Dadaist presentism in Baader's cumulative process and in Arp's, which was subtractive to the point of purism. Quite simply, history took place between Baader's fiction and Arp's eternity.

It is well-known that Dada defended chance as one of the bases of creation. This fits with its devaluation of a certain view of history as objective, determinist, and providential. As Koselleck noted, chance as a historical explanation breaks the chain of determinism and makes room for the new and unexpected. Chance, the ahistorical principle par excellence, streaking into life like a comet, expresses the absurdity of teleology.

These reasons can also account for the enormous differences between Dada and the isms of its time. For John Heartfield, these isms were ersatz versions of philosophy and other previously vanished credos. For his brother, Wieland Herzfelde, they were masks that prevented man from applying the maxim to know thyself. Although the two Marxists rejected isms in the name of transparent truth, not all Dadaists did the same. Huelsenbeck wrote, "The Dadaist is free to adopt any mask; he can represent any 'art movement' since he belongs to no movement."[2] For Huelsenbeck, if Dada imitated all the isms at once, it was in order to bring these successive manifestations of linear history into the simultaneous regime of parody. Dada, in contrast with the isms—whose suffixes contain the autogenesis of the future and which are linguistic condensations of the acceleration of time[3]—chose the equality of the present.[4] Thus, from the moment of its conception, Dada protected itself from the seeds of its own elimination. But the eternity it aspired to had nothing in common with the plus-value of time that, as we have seen, benefited artists of the past. Contrary to the eternity that existed in the detached sphere of Spirit, Dadaist eternity was that of a world of chance, *indifferent* in its intentions, knowing neither good nor evil. And whereas the isms depended on the logical and temporal structure of succession, Dada positioned itself within the simultaneous structure of contradiction, including and above all its own.

Dada was also in opposition to the ism movements such that the artists who met randomly in Zurich opted for the name Dada. Though lacking motivity in time, the word had an astonishing plasticity. It operated like cellular self-division, multiplying infinitely (Dadadadadadada . . . ), including by means of contradiction. And the name Dada was neither masculine nor feminine; it was neuter, because it was undetermined. All in all, Dada recalled a certain royal child who had haunted modern artists,[5] for it was Dada's origin or birth that determined it as neuter. Who, in fact, did invent Dada? Everyone and no one.[6] A host of stories have come down to us about the movement's birth in the Cabaret Voltaire. This birth resembled both an immaculate conception and a bachelor creation. From the latter, Dada drew its repudiation of biological causality, claiming that there could be progeny without a specific progenitor.[7] As for Dada's reference to the Immaculate Conception, it meant that its lineage was uncertain; it also gave it its two-sided nature: both ephemeral and eternal, mortal and immortal. As Huelsenbeck wrote, "Dada came over the Dadaists without their knowing it; it was an immaculate conception, and thereby its profound meaning was revealed to me."[8] Tristan Tzara added:

> A word was born no one knows how DADADADA *we took an oath of friendship* on the new transmutation that signifies nothing, and was the most formidable protest, the most intense armed affirmation of salvation liberty blasphemy mass combat speed prayer tranquility private guerilla negation and chocolate of the desperate.[9]

Dada's immaculate conception was soon after celebrated in the play *Krippenspiel* (Nativity), written by Hugo Ball and performed by all the principal actors of the Cabaret Voltaire. Huelsenbeck later added, "The word Dada was born in February 1916 like Christ in the manger."[10]

For a long time the artist's fertility was the ultimate model of creation. The artist—male, of course—gave birth to his work, which had to prove its own fertility in the eyes of the spectator (remember Kandinsky, for example). This genetic chain was broken with Dada, which, in addition, blurred its genetic codes: it was Dada, the child, that engendered its own parents (as the Dadaists repeated over and over again, no one had foreseen the resonances of their movement); it surpassed the genetic capital that had been transmitted to it, to the point that it effaced itself. The case of Dadaist Francis Picabia is exemplary here. His stated ideal was at each moment to invent a new man but only for the pleasure of forgetting him; to erase, both virtually and physically, the memory of his own works; to become sterile. As for John Heartfield, he invented a fictional lineage, connecting him to a circus family from New Orleans. In short, it was because Dada clearly proclaimed its sterility and fictive genealogy that it accorded itself the right to claim eternity.

The figure of Dada's immaculate conception clearly reveals the movement's complex relations to history. The improbable, inconsistent nature of its birth meant that Dada could never become a historical object among others—or a historical object at all. It became pseudology, legend, and fiction.[11] No doubt this legendary identity suited the vanity of its actors, as they gradually became its historians in their twilight years. But Dada also put a finger on the porous boundaries separating fiction from history. Here too Dada was acutely aware of its time.

# NOTES

## Introduction

1. Oscar Wilde, "The Decay of Lying" (1891), in Wilde, *Intentions*, 42.
2. Woolf, *Orlando*, 235.
3. Woolf, *Orlando*, 307.
4. Woolf, *Orlando*, 219.

## I

1. Huelsenbeck, "En Avant Dada," 40. Originally published as *En Avant Dada: Eine Geschichte des Dadaismus* (Hanover: Paul Steegemann Verlag, 1920).
2. Koselleck, *Futures Past*, 22.
3. See Walter Benjamin, "Experience and Poverty," in Benjamin, *Selected Writings*, 2: 731–36.
4. Of course, postwar Futurism did not create projects for building "cathedrals" as Expressionism did; the reference here is synecdochical. The understanding of apocalypse held by both the Expressionists and the Futurists caused them to envision a total and coherent construction of reality after the catastrophe, even if, for one, the model was in the past, and for the other, in the future.
5. Huelsenbeck, "Dadaco," 99.
6. According to Huelsenbeck, this was in contrast to the Latin nations, whose "tradition" provided succor in troubled times; he referred to France's many "returns to order." This contrast between the weighty tradition of the Latins and the pain-

ful, though potentially productive and even salutary, nonexistence of the Germans as such is a constant in German aesthetic and philosophical thought. See Lacoue-Labarthe, "Histoire et mimésis." The English translation is Lacoue-Labarthe, "History and Mimesis," 209–30.

7. "They overlook that the basic instinct of all the laws in the world has stayed the same" (Huelsenbeck, "Dadaco," 103).

8. Hartog, *Regimes of Historicity*, 17–18.

9. The expression "regimes of historicity" was coined by Hartog, who saw it as a heuristic tool "that can help us reach a better understanding not of time itself—of all times or the whole of time—but principally of moments of crisis of time, as they have arisen whenever the way in which past, present, and future are articulated no longer seems self-evident" (Hartog, *Regimes of Historicity*, 16).

10. Walter Benjamin, "Theses on the Philosophy of History," in Benjamin, *Illuminations*, 261, para. xiv; 262, para. xvi.

11. Huelsenbeck, "Dadaco," 102.

12. Koselleck explained historicism and the philosophy of history as two sides of the same coin: excess of future for one, excess of past—as reaction—for the other.

13. Hausmann, "Dada in Europa," 93.

14. See H. White, "Burden of History."

15. Pinthus, "Rede für die Zukunft," 1: 411. This conception of the past as a dead entity did not entirely dominate Expressionist thought. For Ernst Bloch—whose admiration for the movement is well-known and whose book *The Spirit of Utopia* is in many respects an Expressionist declaration of faith—the past is never entirely dead but rather contains an unachieved potential, which the spirit of utopia must catch hold of.

16. Siegfried Kracauer, "Über den Expressionismus: Wesen und Sinn einer Zeitbewegung" (1918), cited in Frisby, "Social Theory," 104.

17. Pinthus, "Rede für die Zukunft," 411.

18. Pinthus, "Rede für die Zukunft," 411.

19. Pascal, *Pensées*, 16.

20. By "Expressionism" I do not mean only German Expressionism, as is often the case, but rather, in keeping with the different definitions of the term at the time, all the European movements that converged around the principle of the semiotic equivalence of but substantial difference between art and nature; in addition, all these movements were hesitant to make the leap into abstraction. On the term *expressionism*, see

Gordon, "Origin of the Word"; Werenskiold, *Concept of Expressionism*; and von Wiese, "Tempest." On the conflicting, outstretched nature of Expressionism, see Lebensztejn, "Douane-Zoll." On the tension inherent in apocalyptic temporality, see Stavrinaki, "L'empathie *est* l'abstraction"; and Stavrinaki, "Messianic Pains."

21. Marc, "Subscription Prospectus," 47.

22. Kandinsky, "Preface," 257.

23. See Reinhart Koselleck, "'Space of Experience' and 'Horizon of Expectation': Two Historical Categories," in Koselleck, *Futures Past*, 255–75.

24. Kandinsky, *Concerning the Spiritual*, 19.

25. Hilberseimer, "Anmerkungen zur neuen Kunst." A complete English translation of this article can be found in Tafuri, "U.S.S.R.–Berlin 1922," 180n89. On Hilberseimer's interpretation of Dada, see Hays, *Modernism*.

26. Jakobson, "Dada," 39.

27. Huelsenbeck, "En Avant Dada," 27.

28. Ball, *Flight*, 57 (30.III).

29. See the card "George Grosz und John Heartfield wünschen ein frohes Neujahr 1921," reproduced in Bergius, *Dada Triumphs*, Figure 10. In 1922, Georg Scholz clearly formulated the decision to render all modes of plastic expression—whether high or low, ancient or modern—simultaneously: "All the modes of pictorial representation that are available to average Europeans such as ourselves—who are fully conscious of the history of all epochs and all countries, must be taken into account, including kitsch in the sense of pictorial postcards and photographic paintings" (Scholz, "Die wahre Phantasie," 97–98).

30. Nietzsche, *Beyond Good and Evil*, 125.

31. Huelsenbeck, "Introduction," 14.

32. For more on the forms of Dadaist primitivism, a subject that merits extensive exploration, see Ubl, "Wilhelm Worringer"; and Dickerman, "Zurich."

33. Hugo Ball wrote on the subject of Arp's abstraction that "when he advocates the primitive, he means the first abstract sketch that is aware of complexities but avoids them" (Ball, *Flight*, 53 [1.III]). Tristan Tzara wrote, "The influences modern painting hopes to have are among the best: calm, tranquility. Painters are moving toward an impersonal, anonymous art, and see it as medicine against human cruelty, when the angels are liquefied in a Christmas tree" (Tzara, "Note 1," in his *Oeuvres complètes*, 1: 554).

34. "Naïve" in the sense of Friedrich Schiller's essay "On Naïve and Sentimental Poetry" (1795–1796), in Schiller, *Naïve and Sentimental Poetry*.

35. Ball, *Flight*, 65 (2.VI).

36. Ball, *Flight*, 53 (1.III).

37. See Poley, *Hans Arp*.

38. Arp, *Unsern täglichen Traum*, 24.

[39.] "A world of abstract demons engulfed personal expression, swallowed individual faces into masks as tall as towers, swallowed private expression, stripped things of their names, destroyed the Self, and roused oceans of passions against each other" (Ball, "Kandinsky," 14).

40. "This humiliating age has not succeeded in winning our respect. What could be respectable and impressive about it? Its cannons? Our big drum drowns them" (Ball, *Flight*, 61 [14.IV]).

41. See Tzara's poems in his *Oeuvres complètes*, vol. 1.

42. See Stavrinaki, "Hugo Ball."

43. Hal Foster analyzed Hugo Ball's excessive mimesis as a way of adapting to the world. See Foster, "Dada Mime."

44. For more on mimesis as therapy for the traumatic experience of war among the Berlin Dadaists (and Georg Grosz in particular), see Doherty, "We Are All Neurasthenics."

45. Having said that, Jill Lloyd has shown that the primitive and the modern were inextricably linked in the Brücke's works, not only because the modern recognized the primitive as its Other but because it also recognized itself as primitive. See Lloyd, *German Expressionism*. In the same way, formal primitivism—Picasso's being the most striking version—need not be literal; see Kahnweiler, "L'art nègre"; and Bois, "Kahnweiler's Lesson." Finally, we should specify that all primitivism has a functionality.

46. On Carl Einstein's *Negerplastik*, see Zeidler, "Totality"; on the "pact of non-devouring" between the African subject and his/her gods according to Einstein, see Stavrinaki, "Le cauchemar"; on Einstein's interpretation of masks and temporal techniques, see Cheng, "Immanence."

47. See Benson, "Hausmann-Höch."

48. On the relationship between Einstein and Dada in Berlin after the Spartacist revolution, see Fleckner, "The Real Demolished"; Haxthausen, "Bloody Serious"; and Stavrinaki, "Apocalypse primitive."

49. Franz Marc, "Préface du 2ème volume projeté du *Blaue Reiter*," in Marc, *Écrits et correspondances*, 221.

50. For a deeper analysis of the differences between the ontological postulates and techniques of Expressionism and Dadaism, see Stavrinaki, "Dada inhumain"; on the solipsism of Expressionism, see my introduction "Le prédicat selon Marc: de l'ensauvagement à l'ascèse," in Marc, *Écrits et correspondances*, 9–57.

51. "I remember the strange and profound impression made upon me as a child by a plate in an old book that bore the title 'The World Before the Flood.' The plate represented a landscape of the Tertiary period. Man was not yet present. I have often meditated upon the strange phenomenon of this absence of human beings in its metaphysical aspect. Every profound work of art contains two solitudes: one could be called 'plastic solitude,' and is that contemplative beatitude offered to us by genius in construction and formal combination. . . . The second is the life of the *nature morte*, still-life captured not in the sense of pictorial subject, but of the spectral aspect" (de Chirico, "On Metaphysical Art," 89).

52. See Stavrinaki, "Dada inhumain."

53. See Ubl, *Prehistoric Future*.

54. For an analysis of the relationship between Benjamin's theory of the work of art and avant-garde movements, see Michaud, "Autonomie"; and Foster, "Dada Mime."

55. Benjamin, "Das Kunstwerk," 1: 444.

56. Denis Hollier used the notion of use value in his study of the journal *Documents*. The concept is also relevant for describing the Dadaist conception of the work of art. We should add that the Marxist Dadaists reproached Einstein for his confidence in the political efficacy of plastic forms as formative of new consciousness; they expressed this in their criticism of one of Picasso's Cubist collages. See Fleckner, "The Real Demolished." The Dadaist conception of political efficacy is presented later in Chapter III.

57. Hausmann, "Die Kunst und die Zeit," 2: 8.

58. Hausmann, "Die neue Kunst," 1: 184.

59. See Freud, *Beyond the Pleasure Principle*.

60. Draft of a letter from Raoul Hausmann to Hermann Graf Keyserling, dated November 20, 1923, in Hausmann, *Scharfrichter der bürgerlichen Seele*, 190.

61. Here we encounter the problematic of "camouflage," as delineated by Roger Callois beginning in the 1930s and continued in the works of many other thinkers.

62. Hausmann, "Die neue Kunst," 1: 184.

**II**

1. See Adkins, "Erste Internationale Dada-Messe"; Bergius, *Montage*; and Züchner, "Die Erste Internationale Dada-Messe Berlin."

2. See Sawelson-Gorse, *Women in Dada*; Makela, "By Design"; and Schaschke, "Schnittmuster der Kunst."

3. The work's full title was *Der wildgewordene Spiesser Heartfield (Elektromechan. Tatlin-Plastik)*.

4. See Lebensztejn, *L'art de la tache*.

5. Hausmann, "Prothesenwirtschaft," 137–38.

6. See Rabinbach, *Human Motor*.

7. A copy of one of Grosz and Heartfield's earliest photomontages, titled "Wer ist die schönste?" (Who's the Prettiest?) was inserted into the painting; it represents a different "beauty contest," less glorious than the one between war invalids, between the main figures of the government coalition. This photomontage was reprinted on the cover of the February 1919 issue of the short-lived magazine *Jedermann sein eigner Fussball*.

8. See Adkins, "Erste Internationale Dada-Messe."

9. My reading here differs somewhat from Brigid Doherty's in her "Work of Art." The difference lies not so much in our interpretive aims as in our means of arriving at them. Through a meticulous close reading of Rainer Maria Rilke's poem "Archaïscher Torso Apollos" (1908) and drawing on two Dadaists' references to the poet, Doherty tries to read the Dadaist assemblage as a critical interpretation of this sonnet. Whereas Rilke's sonnet is an elegy to the ancient world, which is able to shine through its fragments within interiority, the Dadaist assemblage renounces all hope that contemplation can be of any help, especially contemplation of the ancient world. Thus Doherty shows that what I refer to as the two Dadaists' presentist conception depends on the past, albeit by negation. This elegiac posture seems more palpable to me in Baader's work. As for Grosz and Heartfield, I would like to explore instead the way in which they weave together what I call the actualization of the past and their Marxist deconstruction of the plus-value of this past.

10. Herzfelde, "Introduction," 102.

11. See von Leyden, "History." On the idea of layered time and the importance of the particular in history as they were developed by some influential thinkers of the nineteenth century, see Loriga, *Le petit x*.

12. See Behrens, "Kunst und Technik." See also the analyses by Buddensieg,

*Industriekultur*, 8–95; Cacciari, *Architecture and Nihilism*, 53–55; and Anderson, "Peter Behrens."

13. The expression is Siegfried Kracauer's in his posthumous work on history, where he used it to designate the interpretation of the past according to historians' conjectural interests. See Kracauer, *History*, 62–79.

14. See Nietzsche's second untimely meditation in Nietzsche, *Untimely Meditations*.

15. Baudelaire, "Painter of Modern Life," 9, 3.

16. See Michaud, "L'insensible mélancolie."

17. This is the title of a 1911 painting by Marcel Duchamp. For more on it, see Duve, *Pictorial Nominalism*.

18. See Poggi, *Inventing Futurism*.

19. Filippo Marinetti, cited in Balla and Depero, "Futurist Reconstruction," 209.

20. Herzfelde, "Introduction," 100–101.

21. In "Introduction" Herzfelde presents Orientalism and all other forms of exoticism as amplified expressions of painting's raison d'être: spatiotemporal transposition.

22. Herzfelde, "Introduction," 101.

23. Kessler, *Berlin in Lights*, 91 (March 23, 1919). On the relationship between Count Kessler and John Heartfield, whom Kessler chose to make German cultural-political propaganda films during World War I, see Zervigón, "Political *Struwwelpeter*"; and Zervigón, *John Heartfield*.

24. On Erwin Panofsky's distinction between document and monument, see Panofsky, *Meaning*.

25. Foucault, *Archaeology*, 7.

26. On the image as a matrix of history, see Michaud, "La construction de l'image."

27. On transgression as the duty of art, see Michaud, "Notes."

28. See Schnapp, "Propeller Talk"; Foster, *Prosthetic Gods*, 107–91; and Poggi, "Dreams."

29. See Gough, *Artist as Producer*.

30. Jakobson, "Dada," 35.

31. On the role of film in Dadaism, see Kaes, "Verfremdung als Verfahren."

32. Kracauer, "Photography," 424–25.

33. Von Ranke, "Preface," 57.

34. See Sontag, *On Photography*. Roland Barthes contradicted Kracauer and

Sontag on this point, praising photography's ability to show "what has been." For Barthes, history, which he distinguished from subjective anamnesis, could slip into a detail in a photograph and thus set in motion the work of mourning, whereas for Kracauer photography deadened memory, turning its object into a fossil; a grandmother thus became "an archeological mannikin" (Kracauer, "Photography," 424).

35. Kracauer, "Photography," 432.

36. On Dada's ambiguous relationship with the press and use of the illustrated press, see Bergius, "Dada, the Montage, and the Press."

37. Jakobson was right, and Hanne Bergius developed this idea in his works: Einsteinian relativity was important for Dada, which decided to transpose Einstein's equations from the physical universe to history. For more on Hannah Höch's photocollages, see Bergius, *Montage*.

38. For example, the mannequin appears in Baader's photomontage *Der Verfasser des Buches "Vierzehn Briefe Christi" in seinem Heim* (The Author of the Book "Fourteen Letters of Christ" in His Home), 1920, Museum of Modern Art, New York.

39. See Baader, "Germany's Greatness." On Baader's assemblages, see Foster, "Johannes Baader"; M. White, "Johannes Baader's *Plasto-Dio-Dada-Drama*"; Bergius, *Dada Triumphs*, 231–82 and appendices; and Biro, *Dada Cyborg*, 58–64.

40. Sudhalter, "Johannes Baader." This dissertation is the most complete work on Baader to date and contains a great deal of clarification and information.

41. Michael White's interpretation of Baader's *Plasto-Dio-Dada-Drama* as a description of the fall of Germany and the rise of Baader himself is not convincing. In Dadaism practically nothing operates in two moments; everything is simultaneous and connected, in conformity with the logic of ambivalence and contradiction.

42. Max Weber, "Science as Vocation," in Weber, *Vocation Lectures*, 1–31.

43. For a good documentation of Baader's various actions and publications during his Dadaist years, see Baader, *Das Oberdada*.

44. Baader, "Über private Denkmalspflege," partly translated in Sudhalter, "Johannes Baader," 114.

45. On Wenzel Hablik, see Santomasso, "Origins and Aims"; Hablik and Architectural Association of Great Britain, *Hablik*; Hablik, *Wenzel Hablik*; and Stavrinaki, *La chaîne de verre*.

46. Like Hablik, Baader also had a project for an infinite book, a kind of new gospel that would complete history. *HADO* was to be made of collages, photomontages, the artist's architectural projects, and "vertiginous" press clippings. Often, the

dream of a total work of art goes hand in hand with the dream of a "book"; both are part of a conception of bringing history to a close.

47. See Sudhalter, "Johannes Baader," 114–21.

48. Baader, "Wer ist Dadaist," 134.

49. Quoted in Bergius, *Montage*, 272–81.

50. Apollinaire, *Cubist Painters*, 8.

51. Pinthus, "Rede für die Zukunft," 411.

52. In keeping with this idea, in his photomontage *Reklame für mich: Dada Milchstrasse* (Advertisement for Myself: Dada Milky Way), Baader's face appears as the galactic center of a universe made of press clippings, with numbers and letters mixed together.

53. Kracauer, "Photography," 432.

54. Panofsky, "Original and Facsimile," 337.

## III

1. For a complete account of the heated debate between the Communist Party and the Dadaists, see März, *John Heartfield*. See also McCloskey, *George Grosz*; Doherty, "Work of Art"; Stavrinaki, "Dada inhumain"; and Stavrinaki, "(Sans) parti pris."

2. Grosz and Heartfield, "Art Scab," in Kaes et al., *Weimar Republic Sourcebook*, 484. [Only a portion of Grosz and Heartfield's work appears in this publication; different extracts can be found translated in Grosz, *The Berlin of George Grosz.*—Trans.]

3. See Buck-Morss, "Aesthetics."

4. Grosz and Heartfield, "Art Scab," in Grosz, *Berlin*, 33.

5. Hausmann, "Pamphlet." This essay was originally published in *Der Einzige* 20 (April 20, 1919): 163.

6. "Freilich nur diese; was aber dergestalt ins Wanken gerat, das ist die Autorität der Sache, ihr traditionelles Gewicht" (Benjamin, "Die Kunstwerk," 1: 438).

7. "The situations into which the product of mechanical reproduction can be brought may not touch the actual work of art, yet the quality of its presence is always depreciated. . . . In the case of the art object, a most sensitive nucleus—namely, its authenticity—is interfered with whereas no natural object is vulnerable on that score" (Benjamin, "Work of Art," 221).

8. "Dada is a bluff. Humans are sensory animals, who don't need to be taught what a shudder is. The Dadaist goes beyond his own thirst for sensation and his

own heaviness in his bluff. The bluff is not an ethical principle, but rather practical detoxification" (Hausmann, "Was will der Dadaïsmus in Europa," 95).

9. Raoul Hausmann, "Was ist DADA?" in Hausmann, *Scharfrichter der bürgerlichen Seele*, 107.

10. Raoul Hausmann, "Dada" (April 28, 1918), in Hausmann, *Scharfrichter der bürgerlichen Seele*, 71.

11. Salmon, "Histoire anecdotique," 361.

12. This was also a central idea of Carl Einstein's political and artistic writings from 1912 on.

13. Hilberseimer, "Creation and Evolution," 215. The original manuscript, "Schöpfung und Entwicklung," written in 1922, can be found in the Hilberseimer Archive, Art Institute of Chicago, Series 8/3, Box 1/10.

14. This is despite the fact that, having succumbed to Marxist evolutionism, Benjamin saw Dadaism as a somewhat confused prelude to what film could become if it fully mastered the political potential of its formal methods.

## IV

1. I am referring, of course, to Carl Schmitt's decisionism, which he presented for the first time in his *Political Theology*, written in 1922, the same year as György Lukács's *History and Class Consciousness* (to which I return later in this chapter).

2. Umanskij, "Der Tatlinismus," 12. The book of Umanskij's collected writings is *Neue Kunst in Russland, 1914–1919*.

3. See Raoul Hausmann, notes written on February 2, 1921, in Hausmann, *Courrier Dada*, 87. The "death of art" to which Hausmann refers here is literal: Either art had to disappear (but this was impossible, because according to Hausmann, it was driven by a *Spieltrieb*), or it had to take on the new forms to which its decentering pointed.

4. Kessler, *Berlin in Lights*, 64.

5. Kessler, *Berlin in Lights*, 64. I analyzed this schema, which Wagner inaugurated, of a revolution that takes the form of a return to order in Stavrinaki, "Total Artwork."

6. For a brilliant refutation of this everlasting belief, see Veyne, "Conduites."

7. The artists' exchange of looks is a paradoxical punctum. It is not, as Roland Barthes explains, turned toward a history that goes beyond personal anamnesis but rather is projected into the future.

8. Lukács, *History*, 157.

9. Lukács, *History*, 203–4; emphasis mine.

10. See Stavrinaki, "(Sans) partis pris."

11. Arp et al., "Manifesto Prole Art."

12. Hausmann, "Présentismus," 2: 29.

13. Hausmann, "Présentismus," 2: 25.

14. Saint Augustine, *Confessions*, 267 (XI, 3:17).

15. Derrida, *Grammatology*, 115.

16. Derrida, *Grammatology*, esp. 247–55.

17. Schaschke, *Dadaistische Verwandlungskunst*, 39–60.

18. Hausmann, "Manifest von der Gesetzmässigkeit," 70.

19. See, in particular, Ball, "Der Künstler und die Zeitkrankheit." Here, Ball turns to the Gnostic three-part division between the soma, the soul, and the pneuma.

20. Hausmann, "Présentismus," 2: 29.

21. Many of Carl Einstein's prewar texts developed his views on the poor, in particular, Einstein, "Der Arme" (1913). A text that echoes Hausmann's is Einstein's "On Primitive Art" (1919), in Einstein, "Bloody Serious," 124.

22. "What [the supreme works of beautiful sculpture] lack is the actuality of self-aware subjectivity in the knowing and willing of itself. This defect is shown externally in the fact that the expression of the soul in its simplicity, namely the light of the eye, is absent from the sculptures. The supreme works of beautiful sculpture are sightless, and their inner being does not look out of them as self-knowing inwardness in this spiritual concentration which the eye discloses. This light of the soul falls outside them and belongs to the spectator alone; when he looks at these shapes, soul cannot meet soul nor eye eye" (Hegel, *Hegel's Aesthetics*, 1: 520–21).

23. Hausmann, "Dada in Europa," 93.

24. Hausmann, "Présentismus," 2: 24.

25. Hausmann, "Présentismus," 2: 27.

26. Hausmann, "Die Kunst und die Zeit," 10. On Hausmann's optophonetic projects, see Lista, "Empreintes sonores."

27. Hausmann's presentism was also inspired by Futurist tactilism, a theory developed a bit earlier by Filippo Tommaso Marinetti, who advocated replacing passive contemplation with actions that would allow the primitive communication of thoughts through the skin. See Marinetti, "Tactilism." For an analysis of Hausmann's tactilism through the lens of Benjamin's theory of the work of art, see Wilke, "Tacti(ca)lity Reclaimed."

28. This abstract and rather idealist type of horizontality, which had begun to take shape in artists' imaginations and works around 1920, is thus an antecedent, albeit a very different one, to Surrealism's materialist and primitivist horizontality of the 1930s as it has been analyzed by Rosalind Krauss in her work.

29. Baudelaire, "Salon of 1846," 105.

30. Hausmann, "Présentismus," 2: 29–30.

31. Hausmann agreed with Oswald Spengler regarding the end of all "great convention" (see Spengler, *Decline of the West*, vol. 1, chaps. 7 and 8). The Dadaist artist denounced all vain attempts to resuscitate Great Art, objective and anonymous. He called such attempts *Aufbauismus* (buildingism). See Hausmann, "Puffke propagiert Proletkult," 1: 161–65. But, far from adopting Spengler's declinism, which he had already criticized several times in his writings, Hausmann tried to give another meaning to the term *convention*: the presentist sense of the ordinary, the nonexceptional, to which he thought artists should begin to be more attentive.

32. Hausmann, "Lob des Konventionnelen," 2: 50.

33. Here Hausmann agrees with a classic criticism of the Werkbund and other similar reformist attempts to shape life through art. As we know, Adolf Loos dedicated more than one mordant text to deconstructing such attempts.

**V**

1. Huelsenbeck, "En Avant Dada," 32.

2. Huelsenbeck, "Introduction," 14.

3. See Reinhart Koselleck, "*Neuzeit*: Remarks on the Semantics of Modern Concepts of Movement," in Koselleck, *Futures Past*, 222–54.

4. Dada showed greater lucidity than the "Nunism" behind the journal *Sic*, whose editor and main author, Pierre Albert-Birot, defined it as an "-ism that must survive" (*Sic* 6 [June 1916]; reprinted in Albert-Birot and Lentengre, *Sic*, 43).

5. Merz was a similar version; the "Black Square," a more distant one.

6. Man Ray, "Dadamade," in Man Ray, "From Self Portrait," 43.

7. On the theme of the bachelor machine, I am drawing, of course, on Michel Carrouges's classic work *Les machines célibataires* and Szeemann's catalogue *Junggesellenmaschinen = Les machines célibataires*.

8. Huelsenbeck, "En Avant Dada," 32.

9. Tzara, "Zurich Chronicle," 236.

10. Huelsenbeck, *Dada siegt*, 8.

11. This is how Hausmann justified writing his history of Dada several years later: "A History of Dada reveals the nature of all History. History is nothing but the pseudology of reality created by an individual, nothing more than a bad reflection of complex objectivity in a poor medium" (Hausmann, "Dada est plus que Dada," 17).

# BIBLIOGRAPHY

Adès, Dawn, ed. *The Dada Reader: A Critical Anthology*. Chicago: University of Chicago Press, 2006.

Adkins, Helen. "Erste Internationale Dada-Messe." In *Stationen der Moderne: die bedeutenden Kunstausstellungen des 20. Jahrhunderts in Deutschland*, ed. Eberhard Roters and Bernhard Schulz, 157–69. Berlin: Nicolai? and Berlinische Galerie, 1989.

Albert-Birot, Pierre, and Marie-Louise Lentengre, eds. *Sic: collection complète 1916 à 1919 numéros 1 à 54*. Paris: Jean-Michel Place, 1980.

Anderson, Stanford Owen. "Peter Behrens and the New Architecture of Germany, 1900–1917." Ph.D. diss., Columbia University, 1968.

Apollinaire, Guillaume. *The Cubist Painters*, trans. Peter Read. Berkeley: University of California Press, 2004.

Arp, Hans. *Unsern täglichen Traum: Erinnerungen, Dichtungen und Betrachtungen aus den Jahren 1914–1954*. Zurich: Verlag der Arche, 1955.

Arp, Hans, Tristan Tzara, Theo van Doesburg, Chr. Spengemannd, and Kurt Schwitters. "Manifesto Prole Art." In *The Dada Reader: A Critical Anthology*, ed. Dawn Adès, 296–98. Chicago: University of Chicago Press, 2006.

Baader, Johannes. "Germany's Greatness and Decline." In *The Dada Almanac*, ed. Malcolm Green; trans. Derk Wynand, 97–102. London: Atlas Press, 1993.

———. *Das Oberdada*, ed. Karl Riha. Hofheim: Wolke, 1991.

———. "Über Private Denkmalspflege: Lose Gedanken." *Das Blaubuch* 1, no. 30 (August 1906): 1184–87.

———. "Wer ist Dadaist?" *Freie Strasse* 10 (December 1918). Reproduced in Karl Riha and Jörgen Schäfer, *Dada total: Manifeste, Aktionen, Texte, Bilder* (Leipzig: Reclam Verlag, 1994), 134.

Ball, Hugo. *Flight Out of Time: A Dada Diary*, ed. John Elderfield; trans. Ann Raimes. Berkeley: University of California Press, 1996.

———. "Kandinsky: Conférence à la galerie Dada, Zurich, le 7 avril 1917," trans. Thomas de Kaiser, ed. M. Stavrinaki. *Les Cahiers du Musée National d'Art Modern* 102 (winter 2007/2008): 21–35.

———. "Der Künstler und die Zeitkrankheit." In *Der Künstler und die Zeitkrankheit: Ausgewahlte Schriften*, ed. Hans Burkhard Schlichting, 102–49. Frankfurt am Main: Suhrkamp, 1984.

———. *Der Künstler und die Zeitkrankheit: Ausgewahlte Schriften*, ed. Hans Burkhard Schlichting. Frankfurt am Main: Suhrkamp, 1984.

Balla, Giacomo, and Fortunato Depero. "Futurist Reconstruction of the Universe." In *Futurism: An Anthology*, ed. Lawrence Rainey, Christine Poggi, and Laura Wittman, 209–11. New Haven, CT: Yale University Press, 2009.

Baudelaire, Charles. "The Painter of Modern Life." In Charles Baudelaire, *The Painter of Modern Life and Other Essays*, ed. Jonathan Mayne, 1–40. London: Phaidon, 1964.

———. "The Salon of 1846." In Charles Baudelaire, *Baudelaire: Selected Writings on Art and Artists*, trans. P. E. Charvet, 47–107. Cambridge, UK: Cambridge University Press, 1981.

Behrens, Peter. "Kunst und Technik." *Elektrotechnische Zeitschrift* 31 (June 2, 1910): 552–55.

Benjamin, Walter. *Gesammelte Schriften*, vol. 1, pt. 2, ed. Rolf Tiedemann and Hermann Schweppenhauser. Frankfurt am Main: Suhrkamp, 1974.

———. *Illuminations*, ed. Hannah Arendt; trans. Harry Zohn. New York: Harcourt, Brace & World, 1968.

———. "Die Kunstwerk im Zeitalter seiner technischen Reproduzierbarkeit (Erste Fassung)." In Walter Benjamin, *Gesammelte Schriften*, vol. 1, pt. 2, ed. Rolf Tiedemann and Hermann Schweppenhauser, 444–69. Frankfurt am Main: Suhrkamp, 1974.

———. *Selected Writings*, 4 vols., ed. Michael William Jennings; trans. Rodney Livingston et al. Cambridge, MA: Belknap Press, 1999.

———. "The Work of Art in the Age of Mechanical Reproduction." In *Illuminations*, ed. Hannah Arendt; trans. Harry Zohn, 217–52. New York: Harcourt, Brace & World, 1968.

Benson, Timothy O. "Hausmann-Höch: Begegnung als Künstler." In *Wir wünschen die Welt bewegt und beweglich*, ed. Eva Züchner, 30–44. Berlin: Die Galerie, 1995.

Bergius, Hanne. "Dada, the Montage, and the Press: Catchphrase and Cliché as Basic Twentieth-Century Principles." In *Dada: The Coordinates of Cultural Politics*, ed. Stephen C. Foster, 107–33. New York: G. K. Hall; and London: Prentice Hall International, 1996.

———. *Dada Triumphs! Dada Berlin, 1917–1923: Artistry of Polarities—Montages, Meta-mechanics, Manifestations*. Farmington Hills, MI: G. K. Hall, 2003.

———. *Montage und Metamechanik: Dada Berlin, Artistik von Polaritäten*. Berlin: Mann, 2000.

Bergius, Hanne, and Karl Riha. *Dada Berlin: Texte, Manifeste, Aktionen*. Stuttgart: Reclam, 1977.

Biro, Matthew. *The Dada Cyborg: Visions of the New Human in Weimar Berlin*. Minneapolis: University of Minnesota Press, 2009.

Bloch, Ernst. *The Spirit of Utopia*. Stanford, CA: Stanford University Press, 2000.

Bois, Yve Alain. "Kahnweiler's Lesson." In Yve Alain Bois, *Painting as Model*, 65–97. Cambridge, MA: MIT Press, 1993.

Buck-Morss, Susan. "Aesthetics and Anaesthetics: Walter Benjamin's Artwork Essay Reconsidered." *October* 62 (autumn 1992): 3–41.

Buddensieg, Tilmann. *Industriekultur: Peter Behrens and the AEG, 1907–1914*. Cambridge, MA: MIT Press, 1984.

Burmeister, Hannah, Cornelia Thater-Schulz, Eberhard Roters, and Ralf Höch. *Hannah Höch: eine Lebenscollage*. Berlin: Argon, 1989.

Burmeister, Ralf, ed. *Hannah Höch: aller Anfang ist DADA!* Ostfildern: Hatje Cantz Verlag?; and Berlin: Berlinische Galerie, Landesmuseum für Moderne Kunst, Fotografie und Architektur, 2007.

Cacciari, Massimo. *Architecture and Nihilism: On the Philosophy of Modern Architecture*. New Haven, CT: Yale University Press, 1993.

Carrouges, Michel. *Les machines célibataires*. Paris: Arcanes, 1954.

Cheng, Joyce Suechun. "Immanence Out of Sight: Formal Rigor and Ritual Function in Carl Einstein's 'Negerplastik.'" *Res / Peabody Museum of Archaeology and Ethnology and the Harvard University Art Museums* 55/56 (2009): 87–102.

De Chirico, Giorgio. "On Metaphysical Art" ["Valori Plastici," 1919]. In *Metaphysical Art*, ed. Massimo Carrà, 87–91. New York: Praeger, 1971.

Derrida, Jacques. *Of Grammatology*, trans. Guyatri Spivak. Baltimore: Johns Hopkins University Press, 1988.

Dickermann, Leah. "Zurich." In *Dada*, ed. Laurent Lebon, 988–1014. Cahiers du Musée National d'Art Moderne 88. Paris: Editions du Centre Georges Pompidou, 2005.

Dickerman, Leah, and Matthew S. Witkovsky, eds. *The Dada Seminars*. Washington, DC: Center for Advanced Study in the Visual Arts, 2005.

Doherty, Brigid. "'See: We Are All Neurasthenics!' Or, The Trauma of Dada Montage." *Critical Inquiry* 24, no. 1 (1997): 82–132.

———. "The Work of Art and the Problem of Politics in Berlin Dada." *October* 105 (July 1, 2003): 73–92.

Duplaix, Sophie, and Marcella Lista. "Empreintes sonores et métaphores tactiles: Optophonétique, film et vidéo." In Sophie Duplaix and Marcella Lista, *Sons et lumières: une histoire du son dans l'art du XX<sup>e</sup> siècle*, 63–76. Paris: Centre Pompidou, 2004.

Duve, Thierry de. *Pictorial Nominalism: On Marcel Duchamp's Passage from Painting to the Readymade*. Minneapolis: University of Minnesota Press, 1991.

Einstein, Carl. "Die Arme." In Carl Einstein, *Werke*, ed. Hermann Haarmann and Klaus Siebenhaar, 1: 156–59. Berlin: Fannei & Walz, 1994.

———. "Bloody Serious: Two Texts by Carl Einstein," trans. Charles Haxthausen. *October* 1, no. 105 (2003): 105–18.

Fleckner, Uwe. "The Real Demolished by Trenchant Objectivity: Carl Einstein and the Critical World-View of Dada Verism." In *The Dada Seminars*, ed. Leah Dickerman and Matthew S. Witkovsky, 57–82. Washington, DC: Center for Advanced Study in the Visual Arts, 2005.

Foster, Hal. "Dada Mime." *October* 1, no. 105 (2003): 166–76.

———. *Prosthetic Gods.* Cambridge, MA: MIT Press, 2004.

Foster, Stephen C. *Dada, Dimensions.* Ann Arbor, MI: UMI Research Press, 1985.

———. *Dada, the Coordinates of Cultural Politics.* New York: G. K. Hall, 1996.

———. "Johannes Baader: The Complete Dada." In Stephen C. Foster, *Dada, Dimensions,* 249–71. Ann Arbor, MI: UMI Research Press, 1985.

Foucault, Michel. *The Archaeology of Knowledge,* trans. A. M. Sheridan Smith. New York: Vintage, 1982.

Freud, Sigmund. *Beyond the Pleasure Principle,* trans. James Strachey. New York: Norton, 1975.

Frisby, David. "Social Theory, the Metropolis, and Expressionism." In *Expressionist Utopias: Paradise, Metropolis, Architectural Fantasy,* ed. Timothy O. Benson, 236–63. Los Angeles, CA: Los Angeles County Museum of Art, 1993.

Gordon, Donald E. "On the Origin of the Word 'Expressionism.'" *Journal of the Warburg and Courtauld Institutes* 29 (1966): 368–85.

Gough, Maria. *The Artist as Producer: Russian Constructivism in Revolution.* Berkeley: University of California Press, 2005.

Grosz, George. *The Berlin of George Grosz: Drawings, Watercolours, and Prints 1912–1930,* ed. Frank Whitford. New Haven, CT: Yale University Press, 1997.

Grosz, George, and John Heartfield. "The Art Scab." In George Grosz, *The Berlin of George Grosz: Drawings, Watercolours, and Prints 1912–1930,* ed. Frank Whitford, 32–34. London: Royal Academy of Arts?; and New Haven, CT: Yale University Press, 1997.

———. "The Art Scab." In *The Weimar Republic Sourcebook,* ed. Anton Kaes, Martin Jay, and Edward Dimendberg, 483–86. Berkeley: University of California Press, 1994.

Hablik, Wenzel. *Wenzel Hablik, Architekturvisionen 1903–1920,* ed. Gerda Breuer and Museum Künstlerkolonie Darmstadt. Darmstadt: Häusser, 1995.

Hablik, Wenzel, and Architectural Association of Great Britain. *Hablik, Designer, Utopian, Architect, Expressionist, Artist, 1881–1934.* London: Architectural Association, 1980.

Hartog, François. *Regimes of Historicity: Presentism and Experiences of Time,* trans. Saskia Brown. New York: Columbia University Press, 2015.

Hausmann, Raoul. *Bilanz der Feierlichkeit,* vol. 2, ed. Michael Erlhoff. Munich: Edition Text + Kritik, 1982.

———. *Courrier Dada,* ed. Marc Dachy. Paris: Editions Allia, 2004.

———. "Dada est plus que Dada." In Raoul Hausmann, *Courrier Dada,* ed. Marc Dachy, 15–21. Paris: Editions Allia, 2004.

———. "Dada in Europa." In *The Dada Reader: A Critical Anthology,* ed. Dawn Adès, 92–93. Chicago: University of Chicago Press, 2006.

———. *Documents Raoul Hausmann,* ed. Michel Giroud and Sabine Wolf. Paris: Projectoires, 1975.

———. "Die Kunst und die Zeit." In Raoul Hausmann, *Sieg Triumph Tabak mit*

*Bohnen: Texte bis 1933*, ed. Michael Erlhoff, 2: 7–11. Munich: Edition Text + Kritik, 1982.

———. "Lob des Konventionnelen." In Raoul Hausmann, *Sieg Triumph Tabak mit Bohnen: Texte bis 1933*, ed. Michael Erlhoff, 2: 48–50. Munich: Edition Text + Kritik, 1982.

———. "Manifesto of PREsentism." In *Manifesto: A Century of Isms*, ed. Mary Ann Caws, 164. Lincoln: University of Nebraska Press, 2001.

———. "Manifest von der Gesetzmässigkeit des Lautes." In Raoul Hausmann, *Sieg Triumph Tabak mit Bohnen: Texte bis 1933*, ed. Michael Erlhoff, 2: 69–70. Munich: Edition Text + Kritik, 1982.

———. "Die neue Kunst." In Raoul Hausmann, *Bilanz der Feierlichkeit: Texte bis 1933*, ed. Michael Erlhoff, 1: 179–85. Munich: Edition Text + Kritik, 1982.

———. "Pamphlet Gegen die Weimarische Lebensauffassung." In Raoul Hausmann, *Bilanz der Feierlichkeit: Texte Bis 1933*, ed. Michael Erlhoff, 1: 39–45. Munich: Edition Text + Kritik, 1982.

———. "Présentismus." In Raoul Hausmann, *Sieg Triumph Tabak mit Bohnen: Texte bis 1933*, ed. Michael Erlhoff, 2: 24–30. Munich: Edition Text + Kritik, 1982.

———. "Prothesenwirtschaft." In Raoul Hausmann, *Hurra! Hurra! Hurra! 12 politische Satiren*, ed. Karl Riha, 10–21. Giessen: Anabas, 1992.

———. "Puffke propagiert Proletkult." In Raoul Hausmann, *Sieg Triumph Tabak mit Bohnen: Texte bis 1933*, ed. Michael Erlhoff, 2: 161–65. Munich: Edition Text + Kritik, 1982.

———. *Scharfrichter der bürgerlichen Seele: Raoul Hausmann in Berlin 1900–1933—unveröffentlichte Briefe, Texte, Dokumente aus den Künstler-Archiven der Berlinischen Galerie*, ed. Eva Züchner and Berlinische Galerie. Stuttgart: Hatje, 1998.

———. *Sieg Triumph Tabak mit Bohnen: Texte bis 1933*, 2 vols., ed. Michael Erlhoff. Munich: Edition Text + Kritik, 1982.

———. "Was will der Dadaïsmus in Europa?" In Raoul Hausmann, *Bilanz der Feierlichkeit: Texte bis 1933*, ed. Michael Erlhoff, 1: 60–61. Munich: Text + Kritik, 1982.

Haxthausen, Charles. "Bloody Serious: Two Texts by Carl Einstein." *October* 1, no. 105 (summer 2003): 105–18.

Hays, K. Michael. *Modernism and the Posthumanist Subject: The Architecture of Hannes Meyer and Ludwig Hilberseimer*. Cambridge, MA: MIT Press, 1992.

Hegel, G. W. F. *Hegel's Aesthetics: Lectures on Fine Art*, v. 1, trans. T. M. Knox. Oxford: Clarendon Press, 1975.

Herzfelde, Wieland. "Introduction to the First International Dada Fair," trans. Brigid Doherty. *October* 105 (summer 2003): 93–104.

Hilberseimer, Ludwig. "Anmerkungen zur neuen Kunst." In Will Grohmann and Kunst der Zeit, *Zehn Jahre Novembergruppe*, 52–57. Berlin: Kunst der Zeit, 1928. (Originally published in *Kunst der Zeit* 1–3, no. 3 [1928].)

———. "Creation and Evolution." In K. Michael Hays, *Modernism and the Posthumanist Subject: The Architecture of Hannes Meyer and Ludwig Hilberseimer*. Cambridge, MA: MIT Press, 1992.

Huelsenbeck, Richard, *The Dada Almanach*, ed. Malcolm Green. London: Atlas Press, 1993.

———. "Dadaco." In *The Dada Reader: A Critical Anthology*, ed. Dawn Adès; trans. Kathryn Woodham and Timothy Adès, 99–104. Chicago: University of Chicago Press, 2006.

———. *Dada siegt! Bilanz und Erinnerung*. Hamburg: Nautilus/Nemo Press, 1985.

———. "En Avant Dada: A History of Dadaism." In *The Dada Painters and Poets*, ed. Robert Motherwell; trans. Ralph Mannheim, 23–48. Cambridge, MA: Belknap Press, 1989.

———. "Introduction." In Richard Huelsenbeck, *The Dada Almanach*, ed. Malcolm Green; trans. Derk Wynand, 9–14. London: Atlas Press, 1993.

Jakobson, Roman. "Dada." In Roman Jakobson, *Language in Literature*, ed. Stephen Rudy and Krystyna Pomorska, 34–40. Cambridge, MA: Belknap Press, 1987.

Kaes, Anton. "Verfremdung als Verfahren: Film und Dada." In *Sinn aus Unsinn: Dada International*, ed. Wolfgang Paulsen and Helmut Hermann, 71–83. Bern: Francke, 1982.

Kahnweiler, Daniel Henry. "L'art nègre et le cubisme." In Daniel Henry Kahnweiler, *Confessions esthétiques*, 222–36. Paris: Gallimard, 1963.

Kandinsky, Wassily. *Concerning the Spiritual in Art*, rev. ed., trans. M. T. H. Sadler. London: Dover, 2012.

———. "Preface to the Second Edition." In Wassily Kandinsky, Franz Marc, and Klaus Lankheit, *The Blaue Reiter Almanach*, 257–58. New York: Viking Press, 1974.

Kandinsky, Wassily, Franz Marc, and Klaus Lankheit. *The Blaue Reiter Almanach*. New York: Viking Press, 1974.

Kessler, Harry. *Berlin in Lights: The Diaries of Count Harry Kessler*, ed. Charles Kessler. New York: Grove Press, 2002.

———. *In the Twenties: The Diaries of Harry Kessler*, trans. Charles Kessler. New York: Holt, Rinehart & Winston, 1971.

Koselleck, Reinhart. *Futures Past: On the Semantics of Historical Time*, trans. Keith Tribe. New York: Columbia University Press, 2004.

Kracauer, Siegfried. *History: The Last Things Before the Last*, ed. Paul Oskar Kristeller. New York: Oxford University Press, 1969.

———. "Photography," trans. Thomas Y. Levin. *Critical Inquiry* 19, no. 3 (1993): 421–36.

Lacoue-Labarthe, Philippe. "Histoire et mimésis." In Philippe Lacoue-Labarthe, *L'imitation des modernes*, 86–111. Paris: Galilée, 1986.

———. "History and Mimesis." In *Looking After Nietzsche: Interdisciplinary Encounters with Merleau-Ponty*, ed. Laurence A. Rickels; trans. Eduardo Cadava, 209–30. Albany: SUNY Press, 1990.

Lebensztejn, Jean-Claude. *L'art de la tache: introduction à la nouvelle méthode d'Alexander Cozens*. Paris: Éditions du Limon, 1990.

———. "Douane-Zoll." In *Dresden, Munich, Berlin?: Figures du moderne— L'Expressionnisme en Allemagne?, 1905–1914*, ed. Annie Pérez, Martine Contensou, and Musée d'Art Moderne de la Ville de Paris, 50–56. Paris: Paris-Musées, 1992.

3

3

Lista, Marcella. "Empreintes sonores et métaphores tactiles: Optophonétique, film et video." In *Sons et lumières: une histoire du son dans l'art du XXᵉ siècle*, ed. Sophia Duplaix and Marcella Lista, 63–76. Paris: Centre Pompidou: 2004.

Lloyd, Jill. *German Expressionism: Primitivism and Modernity*. New Haven, CT: Yale University Press, 1991.

Loriga, Sabina. *Le Petit x: de la biographie à l'histoire*. Paris: Éditions du Seuil, 2010.

Lukács, György. *History and Class Consciousness: Studies in Marxist Dialectics*, trans. Rodney Livingstone. London: Merlin Press, 1971.

Makela, Maria Martha. "By Design: The Early Work of Hannah Höch in Context." In Peter W. Boswell, Maria Martha Makela, Carolyn Lanchner, and Kristin Makholm, *The Photomontages of Hannah Höch*, 49–79. Minneapolis: Walker Art Center, 1996.

Man Ray. "From 'Self Portrait.'" In *Surrealist Painters and Poets: An Anthology*, ed. Mary Ann Caws, 41–47. Cambridge, MA: MIT Press, 2002.

Marc, Franz. *Écrits et corréspondances*, ed. Maria Stavrinaki; trans. Thomas de Kaiser. Paris: École Nationale Supérieure des Beaux-Arts, 2006.

———. "Subscription Prospectus." In *German Expressionism: Documents from the End of the Wilhelmine Empire to the Rise of National Socialism*, ed. Rose-Carol Washton Long, 47–49. New York: G. K. Hall, 1993.

Marinetti, Filippo Tommaso. "Tactilism." In *Manifesto: A Century of Isms*, ed. Mary Ann Caws, 197–200. Lincoln: University of Nebraska Press, 2001.

———. "Tactilism: A Futurist Manifesto." In Filippo Tommaso Marinetti, *Critical Writings: New Edition*, ed. Günter Berghaus; trans. Doug Thompson, 370–76. New York: Farrar, Straus & Giroux, 2006.

März, Roland, ed. *John Heartfield, der Schnitt entlang der Zeit: Selbstzeugnisse, Erinnerungen, Interpretationen*. Dresden: Verlag der Kunst, 1981.

McCloskey, Barbara. *George Grosz and the Communist Party: Art and Radicalism in Crisis, 1918 to 1936*. Princeton, NJ: Princeton University Press, 1997.

Michaud, Éric. "Autonomie et distraction." In Éric Michaud, *Histoire de l'art: une discipline à ses frontières*, 13–47. Paris: Éditions Hazan, 2005.

———. "La construction de l'image comme matrice de l'histoire." *Vingtième Siècle* 72, no. 1 (2001): 41–52.

———. "L'insensible mélancolie de la religion et manie de l'art." In Éric Michaud, *La fin du salut par l'image*, 10–23. Paris: Editions Jacqueline Chambon, 1992.

———. "Notes sur la 'déontologie' de l'artiste à l'âge moderne." In *Responsabilités professionnelles et déontologie: les limites éthiques de l'efficacité*, ed. Gilbert Vincent, 245–59. Paris: L'Harmattan, 2002.

Nietzsche, Friedrich. *Beyond Good and Evil / On the Genealogy of Morality*, trans. Adrian Del Caro. Stanford, CA: Stanford University Press, 2014.

———. *Untimely Meditations*, trans. R. J. Hollingdale. Cambridge, UK: Cambridge University Press, 1997.

Panofsky, Erwin. *Meaning in the Visual Arts: Papers in and on Art History*. Garden City, NY: Doubleday, 1955.

———. "Original and Facsimile Reproduction." *Res / Peabody Museum of Archaeology and Ethnology and the Harvard University Art Museums* 57/58 (2010): 330–38.

Pascal, Blaise. *Pensées*, ed. Roger Ariew. Indianapolis: Hackett, 2004.

Pinthus, Kurt. "Rede für die Zukunft." In *Die Erhebung: Jahrbuch für neue Dichtung und Wertung*, ed. Alfred Wolfenstein, 1: 398–42. Berlin: S. Fisher, 1919.

Poggi, Christine. "Dreams of Metallized Flesh: Futurism and the Masculine Body." In Christine Poggi, *Inventing Futurism: The Art and Politics of Artificial Optimism*, 150–80. Princeton, NJ: Princeton University Press, 2009.

———. *Inventing Futurism: The Art and Politics of Artificial Optimism*. Princeton, NJ: Princeton University Press, 2009.

Poley, Stefanie. *Hans Arp: Die Formensprache im plastischen Werk*. Stuttgart: G. Hatje, 1978.

Rabinbach, Anson. *The Human Motor: Energy, Fatigue, and the Origins of Modernity*. Berkeley: University of California Press, 1992.

Saint Augustine. *Confessions*, trans. Garry Wills. New York: Penguin, 2006.

Salmon, André. "Histoire anecdotique du cubisme." In *A Cubism Reader: Documents and Criticism, 1906–1914*, ed. Mark Antliff and Patricia Dee Leighten, 357–67. Chicago: University of Chicago Press, 2008.

Santomasso, Eugene A. "Origins and Aims of German Expressionist Architecture: An Essay into the Expressionist Frame of Mind in Germany, Especially as Typified in the Work of Rudolf Steiner." Ph.D. diss., Columbia University, 1972.

Sawelson-Gorse, Naomi. *Women in Dada: Essays on Sex, Gender, and Identity*. Cambridge, MA: MIT Press, 1998.

Schaschke, Bettina. *Dadaistische Verwandlungskunst: zum Verhältnis von Kritik und Selbstbehauptung in DADA Berlin und Köln*. Berlin: Gebr. Mann, 2004.

———. "Schnittmuster der Kunst: zu Hannah Höchs Prinzipien der Gestaltung." In *Hannah Höch: aller Anfang ist DADA!* ed. Ralf Burmeister, 118–35. Ostfildern: Hatje Cantz Verlag?; and Berlin: Berlinische Galerie, Landesmuseum für Moderne Kunst, Fotografie und Architektur, 2007.

Schiller, Friedrich. *On Naïve and Sentimental Poetry and On the Sublime: Two Essays*, trans. Julius A. Elias. New York: Frederick Ungar, 1967.

Schmitt, Carl. *Political Theology*, trans. George Schwab. Cambridge, MA: MIT Press, 1985.

Schnapp, Jeffrey. "Propeller Talk." *Modernism/Modernity* 1, no. 3 (1994): 153–78.

Scholz, Georg. "Die wahre Phantasie ist der laudernde Spiegel der Gegenwart." *Die Pyramide* 11, no. 14 (1922): 97–98.

Sontag, Susan. *On Photography*. New York: Farrar, Straus & Giroux, 1977.

Spengler, Oswald. *The Decline of the West*, trans. Charles Francis Atkinson. New York: Knopf, 1926.

Stavrinaki, Maria. "Apocalypse primitive: une lecture politique de Negerplastik." *Gradhiva* 14 (2011): 56–77.

———. "Le cauchemar et le rêve: imitations et métamorphoses de l'histoire selon Carl Einstein." *Les Cahiers du Musée National d'Art Moderne / Centre Georges Pompidou* 115 (2011): 34–57.

————. *La chaîne de verre: une correspondance expressionniste.* Paris: Éditions de la Villette, 2009.

————. "Dada inhumain: le sujet et son milieu." *Les Cahiers du Musée National d'Art Modern* 103 (spring 2008): 68–99.

————. "L'empathie est l'abstraction: réflexions sur l'art et la vie de Franz Marc." *Pratiques: Réflexions sur l'Art* 16 (spring 2005): 26–63.

————. "Hugo Ball: le faune et le moine au Cabaret Voltaire." *Retour d'y voir / Musée d'Art Moderne et Contemporain, Genève* 3/4 (2010): 147–71.

————. "Messianic Pains: The Apocalyptic Temporality in Avant-Garde Art, Politics, and War." *Modernism/Modernity* 18, no. 2 (2011): 371–93.

————. "(Sans) partis pris: expressionistes et dadaïstes face à la Révolution spartakiste." In *Artistes et partis: esthétique et politique, 1900–1945,* ed. Maria Stavrinaki and Maddalena Carli, 47–76. Dijon: Les Presses du Réel, 2012.

————. "Total Artwork vs. Revolution: Art, Politics, and Temporalities in the Expressionist Architectural Utopias and the Merzbau." In *The Aesthetics of the Total Artwork: On Borders and Fragments,* ed. Anke K. Finger and Danielle Follett, 253–76. Baltimore: Johns Hopkins University Press, 2011.

Sudhalter, Adrian V. "Johannes Baader and the Demise of Wilhelmine Culture: Architecture, Dada, and Social Critique, 1875–1920." Ph.D. diss., New York University, 2005.

Szeemann, Harald, ed. *Junggesellenmaschinen = Les machines célibataires.* Bern: Kunsthalle, 1975.

Tafuri, Manfredo. "U.S.S.R.–Berlin 1922: From Populism to 'Constructivist International,'" trans. Pellegrino d' Acierno and Robert Connelly. In *Architecture, Criticism, Ideology,* ed. Joan Ockman, 121–81. Princeton, NJ: Princeton Architectural Press, 1985.

Tzara, Tristan. "Note 1 sur quelques peintres." In Tristan Tzara, *Oeuvres complètes,* ed. Henri Béhar, 1: 553–54. Paris: Flammarion, 1996.

————. "Zurich Chronicle." In *The Dada Painters and Poets,* ed. Robert Motherwell, 235–41. Cambridge, MA: Belknap Press, 1989.

Ubl, Ralph. *Prehistoric Future: Max Ernst and the Return of Painting Between the Wars,* trans. Elizabeth Tucker. Chicago: University of Chicago Press, 2013.

————. "Wilhelm Worringer, Hans Arp und Max Ernst bei den Müttern." In *Wilhelm Worringers Kunstgeschichte,* ed. Hannes Böhringer and Beate Söntgen, 119–40. Munich: Wilhelm Fink, 2002.

Umanskij, Konstantin. *Neue Kunst in Russland: 1914–1919.* Munich: Kiepenhauer, 1920.

————. "Der Tatlinismus oder die Maschinenkunst." *Der Ararat* 1, no. 4 (January 1920): 12.

Veyne, Paul. "Conduites sans croyance et oeuvres d'art sans spectateurs." *Diogene* 143 (July 1988): 3–22.

Von Leyden, W. "History and the Concept of Relative Time." *History and Theory* 2, no. 3 (1963): 263–85.

Von Ranke, Leopold. "Preface: *Histories of Romance and Germanic Peoples.*" In *The*

*Varieties of History: From Voltaire to the Present,* 2nd ed., ed. Fritz Stern, 55–60. New York: Vintage, 1973.

Von Wiese, Stephan. "A Tempest Sweeping This World: Expressionism as an International Movement." In *German Expressionism 1915–1925: The Second Generation,* ed. Stephanie Barron and Los Angeles County Museum of Art, 117–23. Los Angeles: Los Angeles County Museum of Art?; and Munich: Prestel, 1988.

Weber, Max. *The Vocation Lectures,* ed. David Owen and Tracy B. Strong; trans. Rodney Livingstone. Indianapolis: Hackett, 2004.

Werenskiold, Marit. *The Concept of Expressionism: Origin and Metamorphoses.* Oslo: Universitetsforlaget; and New York: Columbia University Press, 1984.

White, Hayden V. "The Burden of History." *History and Theory* 5, no. 2 (1966): 111–34.

Wilde, Oscar. *Intentions and The Soul of Man,* ed. Robert Baldwin Ross. Boston: Wyman-Fogg, 1909.

Wilke, Tobias. "Tacti(ca)lity Reclaimed: Benjamin's Medium, the Avant-Garde, and the Politics of the Senses." *Grey Room* 39 (April 1, 2010): 39–55.

Woolf, Virginia. *Orlando.* New York: Harcourt Brace Jovanovich, 1956.

Zeidler, Sebastian. "Totality Against a Subject: Carl Einstein's Negerplastik." *October* 107 (2004): 14–46.

Zervigón, Andrés Mario. *John Heartfield and the Agitated Image: Photography, Persuasion, and the Rise of Avant-Garde Photomontage.* Chicago: University of Chicago Press, 2013.

———. "A 'Political Struwwelpeter'? John Heartfield's Early Film Animation and the Crisis of Photographic Representation." *New German Critique* 107, no. 2 (summer 2009): 5–51.

Züchner, E. "Die Erste Internationale Dada-Messe: Berlin—Eine meta-mechanische Liebeserklärung an Tatlins Maschinenkunst." In *Berlin Moskau, 1900–1950 = Moskva Berlin, 1900–1950,* ed. N. L. Adaskina, Irina Aleksandrovna Antonova, and Jörn Merkert, 118–24. Munich: Prestel, 1995.

# INDEX

The authorized representative in the EU for product safety and compliance is:
Mare Nostrum Group
B.V Doelen 72
4831 GR Breda
The Netherlands

www.ingramcontent.com/pod-product-compliance
Lightning Source LLC
Chambersburg PA
CBHW020922180526
45163CB00007B/2842